Books on Egypt and Chaldæa

EGYPTIAN IDEAS

OF THE

FUTURE LIFE

BY

E. A. WALLIS BUDGE, M.A., Litt.D., D.Lit.

KEEPER OF THE EGYPTIAN AND ASSYRIAN ANTIQUITIES
IN THE BRITISH MUSEUM

WITH EIGHT ILLUSTRATIONS

ISBN: 978-1-63923-669-5

All Rights reserved. No part of this book maybe reproduced without written permission from the publishers, except by a reviewer who may quote brief passages in a review to be printed in a newspaper or magazine.

Printed: February 2023

Published and Distributed By:
Lushena Books
607 Country Club Drive, Unit E
Bensenville, IL 60106
www.lushenabks.com

ISBN: 978-1-63923-669-5

LIST OF ILLUSTRATIONS.

CHAPTER		PAGE
I.	THE CREATION	25
II.	ISIS SUCKLING HORUS IN THE PAPYRUS SWAMP	57
III.	THE SOUL OF OSIRIS AND THE SOUL OF RĀ MEETING IN TATTU. RĀ, IN THE FORM OF A CAT, CUTTING OFF THE HEAD OF THE SERPENT OF DARKNESS	63
IV.	THE JUDGMENT OF THE DEAD IN THE HALL OF MAĀTI	137
V.	THE DECEASED BEING LED INTO THE PRESENCE OF OSIRIS	147
VI.	THE SEKHET-AARU OR "ELYSIAN FIELDS"—	
	(1) FROM THE PAPYRUS OF NEBSENI	177
	(2) FROM THE PAPYRUS OF ANI	181
	(3) FROM THE PAPYRUS OF ANHAI	187

Books on Egypt and Chaldæa

Vol. I.

EGYPTIAN IDEAS OF THE FUTURE LIFE

PUBLISHERS' NOTE.

In the year 1894 Dr. Wallis Budge prepared for Messrs. Kegan Paul, Trench, Trübner & Co. an elementary work on the Egyptian language, entitled "First Steps in Egyptian," and two years later the companion volume, "An Egyptian Reading Book," with transliterations of all the texts printed in it, and a full vocabulary. The success of these works proved that they had helped to satisfy a want long felt by students of the Egyptian language, and as a similar want existed among students of the languages written in the cuneiform character, Mr. L. W. King, of the British Museum, prepared, on the same lines as the two books mentioned above, an elementary work on the Assyrian and Babylonian languages ("First Steps in Assyrian"), which appeared in 1898. These works, however, dealt mainly with the philological branch of Egyptology and Assyriology, and it was impossible in the space allowed to explain much that needed explanation in the other branches of these subjects—that is to say, matters relating to the archæology, history, religion, etc., of the Egyptians, Assyrians, and Babylonians. In answer to the numerous requests which have been made, a series of short, popular handbooks on the most important branches of Egyptology and Assyriology have been prepared, and it is hoped that these will serve as introductions to the larger works on these subjects. The present is the first volume of the series, and the succeeding volumes will be published at short intervals, and at moderate prices.

To

SIR JOHN EVANS, K.C.B., D.C.L., F.R.S.,

ETC., ETC., ETC.

IN GRATEFUL REMEMBRANCE

OF

MUCH FRIENDLY HELP AND ENCOURAGEMENT

PREFACE.

THE following pages are intended to place before the reader in a handy form an account of the principal ideas and beliefs held by the ancient Egyptians concerning the resurrection and the future life, which is derived wholly from native religious works. The literature of Egypt which deals with these subjects is large and, as was to be expected, the product of different periods which, taken together, cover several thousands of years; and it is exceedingly difficult at times to reconcile the statements and beliefs of a writer of one period with those of a writer of another. Up to the present no systematic account of the doctrine of the resurrection and of the future life has been discovered, and there is no reason for hoping that such a thing will ever be found, for the Egyptians do not appear to have thought that it was necessary to write a work of the kind. The inherent difficulty of the subject, and the natural impossibility that different men living in different places and at different times should think alike on matters which must, after all, belong always to the region of faith, render it more than probable that no college of priests, however powerful, was able to formulate a system of beliefs which would be received throughout Egypt by the clergy and the laity alike, and would be copied by the scribes as a final and authoritative work on Egyptian eschatology. Besides this, the genius and structure of the Egyptian language are such as to preclude the possibility of composing in it works of a philosophical or metaphysical character in the true sense of the words. In spite of these difficulties, however, it is possible to collect a great deal of important information on the subject from the funereal and religious works which have come down to us, especially concerning the great central idea of immortality, which existed unchanged for thousands of years, and formed the pivot upon which the religious and social life of the ancient Egyptians actually turned. (From the beginning to the end of his life the Egyptian's chief thought was of the life beyond the grave, and the hewing of his tomb in the rock, and the providing of its furniture, every detail of which was prescribed by the custom of the country, absorbed the best thoughts of his mind and a large share of his worldly goods, and kept him ever mindful of the time when his mummified

Preface. xi

body would be borne to his "everlasting house" in the limestone plateau or hill.

The chief source of our information concerning the doctrine of the resurrection and of the future life as held by the Egyptians is, of course, the great collection of religious texts generally known by the name of "Book of the Dead." The various recensions of these wonderful compositions cover a period of more than five thousand years, and they reflect faithfully not only the sublime beliefs, and the high ideals, and the noble aspirations of the educated Egyptians, but also the various superstitions and childish reverence for amulets, and magical rites, and charms, which they probably inherited from their pre-dynastic ancestors, and regarded as essentials for their salvation. It must be distinctly understood that many passages and allusions in the Book of the Dead still remain obscure, and that in some places any translator will be at a difficulty in attempting to render certain important words into any modern European language. But it is absurd to talk of almost the whole text of the Book of the Dead as being utterly corrupt, for royal personages, and priests, and scribes, to say nothing of the ordinary educated folk, would not have caused costly copies of a very lengthy work to be multiplied, and illustrated by artists possessing the highest skill, unless it had some meaning to them, and was necessary for the attainment by them of the life which is beyond the grave. The "finds" of recent years in Egypt have resulted in the recovery of valuable texts whereby numerous difficulties have been cleared away; and we must hope that the faults made in translating to-day may be corrected by the discoveries of to-morrow. In spite of all difficulties, both textual and grammatical, sufficient is now known of the Egyptian religion to prove, with certainty, that the Egyptians possessed, some six thousand years ago, a religion and a system of morality which, when stripped of all corrupt accretions, stand second to none among those which have been developed by the greatest nations of the world.

E. A. WALLIS BUDGE.

LONDON,
    August 21*st*, 1899.

CONTENTS.

CHAPTER		PAGE
I.	THE BELIEF IN GOD ALMIGHTY	1
II.	OSIRIS THE GOD OF THE RESURRECTION	41
III.	THE "GODS" OF THE EGYPTIANS	84
IV.	THE JUDGMENT OF THE DEAD	110
V.	THE RESURRECTION AND IMMORTALITY	157

EGYPTIAN IDEAS OF THE FUTURE LIFE.

CHAPTER I.

THE BELIEF IN GOD ALMIGHTY.

A STUDY of ancient Egyptian religious texts will convince the reader that the Egyptians believed in One God, who was self-existent, immortal, invisible, eternal, omniscient, almighty, and inscrutable; the maker of the heavens, earth, and underworld; the creator of the sky and the sea, men and women, animals and birds, fish and creeping things, trees and plants, and the incorporeal beings who were the messengers that fulfilled his wish and word. It is necessary to place this definition of the first part of the belief of the Egyptian at the beginning of the first chapter of this brief account of the principal religious ideas which he held, for the whole of his theology and religion was based upon it; and it is also necessary to add that, however

2 ORIGIN OF THE EGYPTIAN RELIGION UNKNOWN.

far back we follow his literature, we never seem to approach a time when he was without this remarkable belief. It is true that he also developed polytheistic ideas and beliefs, and that he cultivated them at certain periods of his history with diligence, and to such a degree that the nations around, and even the stranger in his country, were misled by his actions, and described him as a polytheistic idolater. But notwithstanding all such departures from observances, the keeping of which befitted those who believed in God and his unity, this sublime idea was never lost sight of; on the contrary, it is reproduced in the religious literature of all periods. Whence came this remarkable characteristic of the Egyptian religion no man can say, and there is no evidence whatsoever to guide us in formulating the theory that it was brought into Egypt by immigrants from the East, as some have said, or that it was a natural product of the indigenous peoples who formed the population of the valley of the Nile some ten thousand years ago, according to the opinion of others. All that is known is that it existed there at a period so remote that it is useless to attempt to measure by years the interval of time which has elapsed since it grew up and established itself in the minds of men, and that it is exceedingly doubtful if we shall ever have any very definite knowledge on this interesting point.

But though we know nothing about the period of

the origin in Egypt of the belief in the existence of an almighty God who was One, the inscriptions show us that this Being was called by a name which was something like *Neter*,[1] the picture sign for which was an axe-head, made probably of stone, let into a long wooden handle. The coloured picture character shews that the axe-head was fastened into the handle by thongs of leather or string, and judging by the general look of the object it must have been a formidable weapon in strong, skilled hands. A theory has recently been put forward to the effect that the picture character represents a stick with a bit of coloured rag tied to the top, but it will hardly commend itself to any archaeologist. The lines which cross the side of the axe-head represent string or strips of leather, and indicate that it was made of stone which, being brittle, was liable to crack; the picture characters which delineate the object in the latter dynasties shew that metal took the place of the stone axe-head, and being tough the new substance needed no support. The mightiest man in the prehistoric days was he who had the best weapon, and knew how to wield it with the greatest effect; when the prehistoric hero of many fights and victories passed to his rest, his own or a similar weapon was buried with him to enable him to wage war successfully in the next world. The

[1] There is no *e* in Egyptian, and this vowel is added merely to make the word pronounceable.

4 DERIVATION FROM COPTIC IMPOSSIBLE.

mightiest man had the largest axe, and the axe thus became the symbol of the mightiest man. As he, by reason of the oft-told narrative of his doughty deeds at the prehistoric camp fire at eventide, in course of time passed from the rank of a hero to that of a god, the axe likewise passed from being the symbol of a hero to that of a god. Far away back in the early dawn of civilization in Egypt, the object which I identify as an axe may have had some other signification, but if it had, it was lost long before the period of the rule of the dynasties in that country.

Passing now to the consideration of the meaning of the name for God, *neter*, we find that great diversity of opinion exists among Egyptologists on the subject. Some, taking the view that the equivalent of the word exists in Coptic, under the form of *Nuti*, and because Coptic is an ancient Egyptian dialect, have sought to deduce its meaning by seeking in that language for the root from which the word may be derived. But all such attempts have had no good result, because the word *Nuti* stands by itself, and instead of being derived from a Coptic root is itself the equivalent of the Egyptian *neter*,[1] and was taken over by the translators of the Holy Scriptures from that language to express the words "God" and "Lord." The Coptic root *nomti* cannot in any way be connected with *nuti*, and the attempt to prove that the two are related was only

---

[1] The letter *r* has dropped out in Coptic through phonetic decay.

THE MEANING OF NETER.

made with the view of helping to explain the fundamentals of the Egyptian religion by means of Sanskrit and other Aryan analogies. It is quite possible that the word *neter* means "strength," "power," and the like, but these are only some of its derived meanings, and we have to look in the hieroglyphic inscriptions for help in order to determine its most probable meaning. The eminent French Egyptologist, E. de Rougé, connected the name of God, *neter*, with the other word *neter*, "renewal" or "renovation," and it would, according to his view, seem as if the fundamental idea of God was that of the Being who had the power to renew himself perpetually—or in other words, "self-existence." The late Dr. H. Brugsch partly accepted this view, for he defined *neter* as being "the active power which produces and creates things in regular recurrence; which bestows new life upon them, and gives back to them their youthful vigour."[1] There seems to be no doubt that, inasmuch as it is impossible to find any one word which will render *neter* adequately and satisfactorily, "self-existence" and "possessing the power to renew life indefinitely," may together be taken as the equivalent of *neter* in our own tongue. M. Maspero combats rightly the attempt to make "strong" the meaning of *neter* (masc.), or *neterit* (fem.) in these words: "In the expressions 'a town *neterit* 'an arm *neteri*,' . . . is it certain that 'a strong city,'

[1] *Religion und Mythologie*, p. 93.

6 THE MEANING OF NETER.

'a strong arm,' give us the primitive sense of *neter*? When among ourselves one says 'divine music,' 'a piece of divine poetry,' 'the divine taste of a peach,' 'the divine beauty of a woman,' [the word] divine is a hyperbole, but it would be a mistake to declare that it originally meant 'exquisite' because in the phrases which I have imagined one could apply it as 'exquisite music,' 'a piece of exquisite poetry,' 'the exquisite taste of a peach,' 'the exquisite beauty of a woman.' Similarly, in Egyptian, 'a town *neterit*' is 'a divine town;' 'an arm *neteri*' is 'a divine arm,' and *neteri* is employed metaphorically in Egyptian as is [the word] 'divine' in French, without its being any more necessary to attribute to [the word] *neteri* the primitive meaning of 'strong,' than it is to attribute to [the word] 'divine' the primitive meaning of 'exquisite.'"[1] It may be, of course, that *neter* had another meaning which is now lost, but it seems that the great difference between God and his messengers and created things is that he is the Being who is self-existent and immortal, whilst they are not self-existent and are mortal.

Here it will be objected by those who declare that the ancient Egyptian idea of God is on a level with that evolved by peoples and tribes who stand comparatively little removed from very intelligent animals, that such high conceptions as self-existence and immortality belong to a people who are already on a

[1] *La Mythologie Égyptienne*, p. 215.

PRIMITIVE IDEA OF GOD.   7

high grade of development and civilization. This is precisely the case with the Egyptians when we first know them. As a matter of fact, we know nothing of their ideas of God before they developed sufficiently to build the monuments which we know they built, and before they possessed the religion, and civilization, and complex social system which their writings have revealed to us. In the remotest prehistoric times it is probable that their views about God and the future life were little better than those of the savage tribes, now living, with whom some have compared them. The primitive god was an essential feature of the family, and the fortunes of the god varied with the fortunes of the family; the god of the city in which a man lived was regarded as the ruler of the city, and the people of that city no more thought of neglecting to provide him with what they considered to be due to his rank and position than they thought of neglecting to supply their own wants. In fact the god of the city became the centre of the social fabric of that city, and every inhabitant thereof inherited automatically certain duties, the neglect of which brought stated pains and penalties upon him. The remarkable peculiarity of the Egyptian religion is that the primitive idea of the god of the city is always cropping up in it, and that is the reason why we find semi-savage ideas of God side by side with some of the most sublime conceptions, and it of course underlies

8 EXAMPLES OF THE USE OF NETER.

all the legends of the gods wherein they possess all the attributes of men and women. The Egyptian in his semi-savage state was neither better nor worse than any other man in the same stage of civilization, but he stands easily first among the nations in his capacity for development, and in his ability for evolving conceptions concerning God and the future life, which are claimed as the peculiar product of the cultured nations of our time.

We must now, however, see how the word for God, *neter*, is employed in religious texts and in works which contain moral precepts. In the text of Unas,[1] a king who reigned about B.C. 3300, we find the passage :—" That which is sent by thy *ka* cometh to thee, that which is sent by thy father cometh to thee, that which is sent by Rā cometh to thee, and it arriveth in the train of thy Rā. Thou art pure, thy bones are the gods and the goddesses of heaven, thou existest at the side of God, thou art unfastened, thou comest forth towards thy soul, for every evil word (or thing) which hath been written in the name of Unas hath been done away." And, again, in the text of Teta,[2] in the passage which refers to the place in the eastern part of heaven " where the gods give birth unto themselves, where that to which they give birth is born, and where they renew their youth," it is said of this king, " Teta standeth up in the form of

[1] Ed. Maspero, *Pyramides de Saqqarah*, p. 25.   [2] *Ibid.*, p. 113.

the star ... he weigheth words (*or* trieth deeds), and behold God hearkeneth unto that which he saith." Elsewhere[1] in the same text we read, " Behold, Teta hath arrived in the height of heaven, and the *henmemet* beings have seen him ; the Semketet[2] boat knoweth him, and it is Teta who saileth it, and the Mãntchet[3] boat calleth unto him, and it is Teta who bringeth it to a standstill. Teta hath seen his body in the Semketet boat, he knoweth the uraeus which is in the Mãntchet boat, and God hath called him in his name ... and hath taken him in to Rã." And again[4] we have: "Thou hast received the form (*or* attribute) of God, and thou hast become great therewith before the gods"; and of Pepi I., who reigned about B.C. 3000, it is said, "This Pepi is God, the son of God."[5]

Now in these passages the allusion is to the supreme Being in the next world, the Being who has the power to invoke and to obtain a favourable reception for the deceased king by Rã, the Sun-god, the type and symbol of God. It may, of course, be urged that the word *neter* here refers to Osiris, but it is not customary to speak of this god in such a way in the texts; and even if we admit that it does, it only shows that the powers of God have been attributed to Osiris, and that he was believed to occupy the position in

---

[1] Ed. Maspero, *Pyramides de Saqqarah*, p. 111.
[2] The morning boat of the sun. [3] The evening boat of the sun.
[4] *Ibid.*, p. 150. [5] *Ibid.*, p. 222.

respect of Rā and the deceased which the supreme Being himself occupied. In the last two extracts given above we might read "a god" instead of "God," but there is no object in the king receiving the form or attribute of a nameless god; and unless Pepi becomes the son of God, the honour which the writer of that text intends to ascribe to the king becomes little and even ridiculous.

Passing from religious texts to works containing moral precepts, we find much light thrown upon the idea of God by the writings of the early sages of Egypt. First and foremost among these are the "Precepts of Kaqemna" and the "Precepts of Ptah-hetep," works which were composed as far back as B.C. 3000. The oldest copy of them which we possess is, unfortunately, not older than B.C. 2500, but this fact in no way affects our argument. These "precepts" are intended to form a work of direction and guidance for a young man in the performance of his duty towards the society in which he lived and towards his God. It is only fair to say that the reader will look in vain in them for the advice which is found in writings of a similar character composed at a later period; but as a work intended to demonstrate the "whole duty of man" to the youth of the time when the Great Pyramid was still a new building, these "precepts" are very remarkable. The idea of God held by Ptah-hetep is illustrated by the following passages:—

1. "Thou shalt make neither man nor woman to be afraid, for God is opposed thereto; and if any man shall say that he will live thereby, He will make him to want bread."

2. "As for the nobleman who possesseth abundance of goods, he may act according to his own dictates; and he may do with himself that which he pleaseth; if he will do nothing at all, that also is as he pleaseth. The nobleman by merely stretching out his hand doeth that which mankind (*or* a person) cannot attain to; but inasmuch as the eating of bread is according to the plan of God, this cannot be gainsaid."

3. "If thou hast ground to till, labour in the field which God hath given thee; rather than fill thy mouth with that which belongeth to thy neighbours it is better to terrify him that hath possessions [to give them unto thee]."

4. "If thou abasest thyself in the service of a perfect man, thy conduct shall be fair before God."

5. "If thou wouldst be a wise man, make thou thy son to be pleasing unto God."

6. "Satisfy those who depend upon thee as far as thou art able so to do; this should be done by those whom God hath favoured."

7. "If, having been of no account, thou hast become great; and if, having been poor, thou hast become rich; and if thou hast become governor of the city, be not hard-hearted on account of thy advancement, because

thou hast become merely the guardian of the things which God hath provided."

8 "What is loved of God is obedience; God hateth disobedience."

9. "Verily a good son is of the gifts of God."[1]

The same idea of God, but considerably amplified in some respects, may be found in the *Maxims of Khensu-hetep*, a work which was probably composed during the XVIIIth dynasty. This work has been studied in detail by a number of eminent Egyptologists, and though considerable difference of opinion has existed among them in respect of details and grammatical niceties, the general sense of the maxims has been clearly established. To illustrate the use of the word *neter*, the following passages have been chosen from it:[2]—

1. "God magnifieth his name."

2. "What the house of God hateth is much speaking. Pray thou with a loving heart all the petitions which are in secret. He will perform thy business, he will hear that which thou sayest and will accept thine offerings."

3. "God decreeth the right."

[1] The text was published by Prisse d'Avennes, entitled *Facsimile d'un papyrus Égyptien en caractères hiératiques*, Paris, 1847. For a translation of the whole work, see Virey, *Études sur le Papyrus Prisse*, Paris, 1887.

[2] They are given with interlinear transliteration and translation in my *Papyrus of Ani*, p. lxxxv. ff., where references to the older literature on the subject will be found.

GOD AND "GODS."

4. "When thou makest an offering unto thy God, guard thou against the things which are an abomination unto him. Behold thou his plans with thine eye, and devote thyself to the adoration of his name. He giveth souls unto millions of forms, and him that magnifieth him doth he magnify."

5. "If thy mother raise her hands to God he will hear her prayers [and rebuke thee]."

7. "Give thyself to God, and keep thou thyself daily for God."

Now, although the above passages prove the exalted idea which the Egyptians held of the supreme Being, they do not supply us with any of the titles and epithets which they applied to him; for these we must have recourse to the fine hymns and religious meditations which form so important a part of the "Book of the Dead." But before we quote from them, mention must be made of the *neteru, i.e.*, the beings or existences which in some way partake of the nature or character of God, and are usually called "gods." The early nations that came in contact with the Egyptians usually misunderstood the nature of these beings, and several modern Western writers have done the same. When we examine these "gods" closely, they are found to be nothing more nor less than forms, or manifestations, or phases, or attributes, of one god, that god being Rā the Sun-god, who, it must be remembered, was the type and symbol of God. Nevertheless, the worship of the *neteru* by the Egyptians has been made the base of the charge of "gross idolatry" which has been brought against them, and they have been represented by some as being on the low intellectual level of savage tribes. It is certain that from the earliest times one of the greatest tendencies of the Egyptian religion was towards monotheism, and this tendency may be observed in all important texts down to the latest period; it is also certain that a kind of polytheism existed in Egypt side by side with monotheism from very early times. Whether monotheism or polytheism be the older, it is useless in our present state of knowledge to attempt to enquire. According to Tiele, the religion of Egypt was at the beginning polytheistic, but developed in two opposite directions: in the one direction gods were multiplied by the addition of local gods, and in the other the Egyptians drew nearer and nearer to monotheism.[1] Dr. Wiedemann takes the view that three main elements may be recognized in the Egyptian religion: (1) A solar monotheism, that is to say one god, the creator of the universe, who manifests his power especially in the sun and its operations; (2) A cult of the regenerating power of nature, which expresses itself in the adoration of ithyphallic gods, of fertile goddesses, and of a series

[1] *Geschiedenis van den Godsdienst in de Oudheid*, Amsterdam, 1893, p. 25. A number of valuable remarks on this subject are given by Lieblein in *Egyptian Religion*, p. 10.

of animals and of various deities of vegetation; (3) A perception of an anthropomorphic divinity, the life of whom in this world and in the world beyond this was typical of the ideal life of man[1]—this last divinity being, of course, Osiris. But here again, as Dr. Wiedemann says, it is an unfortunate fact that all the texts which we possess are, in respect of the period of the origin of the Egyptian religion, comparatively late, and therefore in them we find these three elements mixed together, along with a number of foreign matters, in such a way as to make it impossible to discover which of them is the oldest. No better example can be given of the loose way in which different ideas about a god and God are mingled in the same text than the "Negative Confession" in the hundred and twenty-fifth chapter of the Book of the Dead. Here, in the oldest copies of the passages known, the deceased says, "I have not cursed God" (L 38), and a few lines after (1. 42) he adds, "I have not thought scorn of the god living in my city." It seems that here we have indicated two different layers of belief, and that the older is represented by the allusion to the "god of the city," in which case it would go back to the time when the Egyptian lived in a very primitive fashion. If we assume that God (who is mentioned in line 38) is Osiris, it does not do away with the fact that he was regarded as a being entirely different from the "god of

---

[1] *Le Livre des Morts* (Review in *Muséon*, Tom. xiii. 1893).

the city" and that he was of sufficient importance to have one line of the "Confession" devoted to him. The Egyptian saw no incongruity in setting references to the "gods" side by side with allusions to a god whom we cannot help identifying with the Supreme Being and the Creator of the world; his ideas and beliefs have, in consequence, been sadly misrepresented, and by certain writers he has been made an object of ridicule. What, for example, could be a more foolish description of Egyptian worship than the following? "Who knows not, O Volusius of Bithynia, the sort of monsters Egypt, in her infatuation, worships. One part venerates the crocodile; another trembles before an ibis gorged with serpents. The image of a sacred monkey glitters in gold, where the magic chords sound from Memnon broken in half, and ancient Thebes lies buried in ruins, with her hundred gates. In one place they venerate sea-fish, in another river-fish; there, whole towns worship a dog: no one Diana. It is an impious act to violate or break with the teeth a leek or an onion. O holy nations! whose gods grow for them in their gardens! Every table abstains from animals that have wool: it is a crime there to kill a kid. But human flesh is lawful food."[1]

[1] Juvenal, Satire XV. (Evans' translation in Bohn's Series, p. 180). Led astray by Juvenal, our own good George Herbert (*Church Militant*) wrote:—

"At first he (*i.e.*, Sin) got to Egypt, and did sow
Gardens of gods, which every year did grow

The epithets which the Egyptians applied to their gods also bear valuable testimony concerning the ideas which they held about God. We have already said that the "gods" are only forms, manifestations, and phases of Rā, the Sun-god, who was himself the type and symbol of God, and it is evident from the nature of these epithets that they were only applied to the "gods" because they represented some quality or attribute which they would have applied to God had it been their custom to address Him. Let us take as examples the epithets which are applied to Hāpi the god of the Nile. The beautiful hymn[1] to this god opens as follows:—

"Homage to thee, O Hāpi! Thou comest forth in this land, and dost come in peace to make Egypt to live, O thou hidden one, thou guide of the darkness whensoever it is thy pleasure to be its guide. Thou waterest the fields which Rā hath created, thou makest all animals to live, thou makest the land to drink

> Fresh and fine deities. They were at great cost,
> Who for a god clearly a sallet lost.
> Ah, what a thing is man devoid of grace,
> Adoring garlic with an humble face,
> Begging his food of that which he may eat,
> Starving the while he worshippeth his meat!
> Who makes a root his god, how low is he,
> If God and man be severed infinitely!
> What wretchedness can give him any room,
> Whose house is foul, while he adores his broom?

[1] The whole hymn has been published by Maspero in *Hymne au Nil*, Paris, 1868.

without ceasing; thou descendest the path of heaven, thou art the friend of meat and drink, thou art the giver of the grain, and thou makest every place of work to flourish, O Ptah! . . . If thou wert to be overcome in heaven the gods would fall down headlong, and mankind would perish. Thou makest the whole earth to be opened (*or* ploughed up) by the cattle, and prince and peasant lie down to rest. . . . His disposition (*or* form) is that of Khnemu; when he shineth upon the earth there is rejoicing, for all people are glad, the mighty man (?) receiveth his meat, and every tooth hath food to consume."

After praising him for what he does for mankind and beasts, and for making the herb to grow for the use of all men, the text says:—

"He cannot be figured in stone; he is not to be seen in the sculptured images upon which men place the united crowns of the South and the North furnished with uraei; neither works nor offerings can be made to him; and he cannot be made to come forth from his secret place. The place where he liveth is unknown; he is not to be found in inscribed shrines; there existeth no habitation which can contain him; and thou canst not conceive his form in thy heart."

First we notice that Hāpi is addressed by the names of Ptah and Khnemu, not because the writer thought these three gods were one, but because Hāpi as the great supplier of water to Egypt became, as it were,

THE UNITY OF GOD.

a creative god like Ptah and Khnemu. Next we see that it is stated to be impossible to depict him in paintings, or even to imagine what his form may be, for he is unknown and his abode cannot be found, and no place can contain him. But, as a matter of fact, several pictures and sculptures of Hāpi have been preserved, and we know that he is generally depicted in the form of two gods; one has upon his head a papyrus plant, and the other a lotus plant, the former being the Nile-god of the South, and the latter the Nile-god of the North. Elsewhere he is portrayed in the form of a large man having the breasts of a woman. It is quite clear, then, that the epithets which we have quoted are applied to him merely as a form of God. In another hymn, which was a favourite in the XVIIIth and XIXth dynasties, Hāpi is called "One," and is said to have created himself; but as he is later on in the text identified with Rā the epithets which belong to the Sun-god are applied to him. The late Dr. H. Brugsch collected[1] a number of the epithets which are applied to the gods, from texts of all periods; and from these we may see that the ideas and beliefs of the Egyptians concerning God were almost identical with those of the Hebrews and Muhammadans at later periods. When classified these epithets read thus:—

"God is One and alone, and none other existeth

[1] *Religion und Mythologie*, pp. 96-99.

with Him; God is the One, the One Who hath made all things.

"God is a spirit, a hidden spirit, the spirit of spirits, the great spirit of the Egyptians, the divine spirit.

"God is from the beginning, and He hath been from the beginning; He hath existed from of old and was when nothing else had being. He existed when nothing else existed, and what existeth He created after He had come into being. He is the father of beginnings.

"God is the eternal One, He is eternal and infinite; and endureth for ever and aye; He hath endured for countless ages, and He shall endure to all eternity.

"God is the hidden Being, and no man hath known His form. No man hath been able to seek out His likeness; He is hidden from gods and men, and He is a mystery unto His creatures.

"No man knoweth how to know Him. His name remaineth hidden; His name is a mystery unto His children. His names are innumerable, they are manifold and none knoweth their number.

"God is truth, and He liveth by truth, and He feedeth thereon. He is the King of truth, He resteth upon truth, He fashioneth truth, and He executeth truth throughout all the world.

"God is life, and through Him only man liveth. He giveth life to man, and He breatheth the breath of life into his nostrils.

"God is father and mother, the father of fathers,

and the mother of mothers. He begetteth, but was never begotten; He produceth, but was never produced He begat Himself and produced Himself. He createth, but was never created; He is the maker of His own form, and the fashioner of His own body.

"God Himself is existence, He liveth in all things, and liveth upon all things. He endureth without increase or diminution, He multiplieth Himself millions of times, and He possesseth multitudes of forms and multitudes of members.

"God hath made the universe, and He hath created all that therein is: He is the Creator of what is in this world, of what was, of what is, and of what shall be. He is the Creator of the world, and it was He Who fashioned it with His hands before there was any beginning; and He stablished it with that which went forth from Him. He is the Creator of the heavens and the earth; the Creator of the heavens, and the earth, and the deep; the Creator of the heavens, and the earth, and the deep, and the waters, and the mountains. God hath stretched out the heavens and founded the earth. What His heart conceived came to pass straightway, and when He had spoken His word came to pass, and it shall endure for ever.

"God is the father of the gods, and the father of the father of all deities; He made His voice to sound, and the deities came into being, and the gods sprang into existence after He had spoken with His mouth. He formed mankind and fashioned the gods. He is the great Master, the primeval Potter Who turned men and gods out of His hands, and He formed men and gods upon a potter's table.

"The heavens rest upon His head, and the earth supporteth His feet; heaven hideth His spirit, the earth hideth His form, and the underworld shutteth up the mystery of Him within it. His body is like the air, heaven resteth upon His head, and the new inundation [of the Nile] containeth His form.

"God is merciful unto those who reverence Him, and He heareth him that calleth upon Him. He protecteth the weak against the strong, and He heareth the cry of him that is bound in fetters; He judgeth between the mighty and the weak. God knoweth him that knoweth Him, He rewardeth him that serveth Him, and He protecteth him that followeth Him."

We have now to consider the visible emblem, and the type and symbol of God, namely the Sun-god Rā, who was worshipped in Egypt in prehistoric times. According to the writings of the Egyptians, there was a time when neither heaven nor earth existed, and when nothing had being except the boundless primeval[1] water, which was, however, shrouded with thick darkness. In this condition the primeval water remained for a considerable time, notwithstanding that it contained within it the germs of the things which afterwards

[1] See Brugsch, *Religion*, p. 101.

THE CREATION.

came into existence in this world, and the world itself. At length the spirit of the primeval water felt the desire for creative activity, and having uttered the word, the world sprang straightway into being in the form which had already been depicted in the mind of the spirit before he spake the word which resulted in its creation. The next act of creation was the formation of a germ, or egg, from which sprang Rā, the Sun-god, within whose shining form was embodied the almighty power of the divine spirit.

Such was the outline of creation as described by the late Dr. H. Brugsch, and it is curious to see how closely his views coincide with a chapter in the *Papyrus of Nesi Amsu* preserved in the British Museum.[1] In the third section of this papyrus we find a work which was written with the sole object of overthrowing Āpep, the great enemy of Rā, and in the composition itself we find two versions of the chapter which describes the creation of the earth and all things therein. The god Neb-er-tcher is the speaker, and he says:—

"I evolved the evolving of evolutions. I evolved myself under the form of the evolutions of the god Khepera, which were evolved at the beginning of all time. I evolved with the evolutions of the god Khepera; I evolved by the evolution of evolutions—

---

[1] No. 10,188. See my transcript and translation of the whole papyrus in *Archæologia*, vol. 52, London, 1891.

that is to say, I developed myself from the primeval matter which I made, I developed myself out of the primeval matter. My name is Ausares (Osiris), the germ of primeval matter. I have wrought my will wholly in this earth, I have spread abroad and filled it, I have strengthened it [with] my hand. I was alone, for nothing had been brought forth; I had not then emitted from myself either Shu or Tefnut. I uttered my own name, as a word of power, from my own mouth, and I straightway evolved myself. I evolved myself under the form of the evolutions of the god Khepera, and I developed myself out of the primeval matter which has evolved multitudes of evolutions from the beginning of time. Nothing existed on this earth then, and I made all things. There was none other who worked with me at that time. I performed all evolutions there by means of that divine Soul which I fashioned there, and which had remained inoperative in the watery abyss. I found no place there whereon to stand. But I was strong in my heart, and I made a foundation for myself, and I made everything which was made. I was alone. I made a foundation for my heart (*or* will), and I created multitudes of things which evolved themselves like unto the evolutions of the god Khepera, and their offspring came into being from the evolutions of their births. I emitted from myself the gods Shu and Tefnut, and from being One I became Three; they

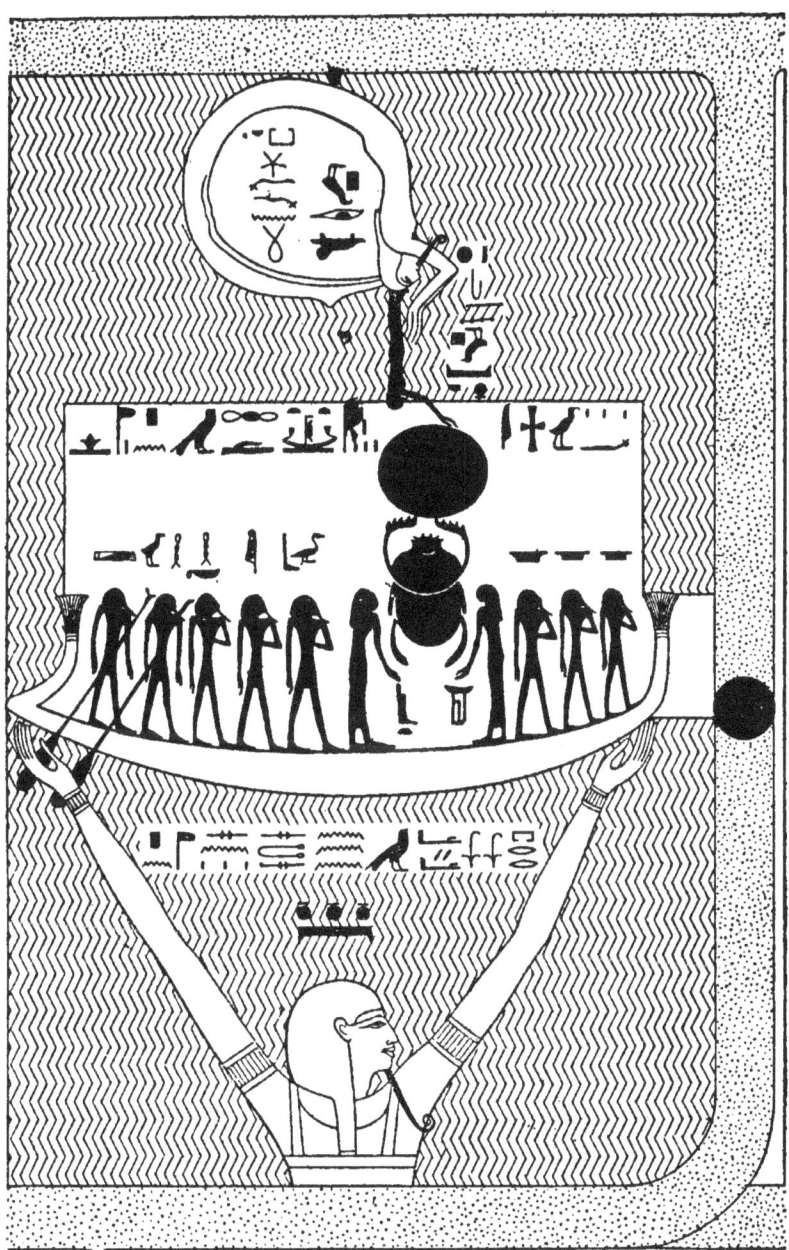

THE CREATION.

The god Nu rising out of the primeval water and bearing in his hands the boat of Râ, the Sun-god, who is accompanied by a number of deities In the upper portion of the scene is the region of the underworld which is enclosed by the body of Osiris, on whose head stands the goddess Nut with arms stretched out to receive the disk of the sun.

sprang from me, and came into existence in this earth.
.... Shu and Tefnut brought forth Seb and Nut, and Nut brought forth Osiris, Horus-kheut-an-maa, Sut, Isis, and Nephthys at one birth."

The fact of the existence of two versions of this remarkable Chapter proves that the composition is much older than the papyrus[1] in which it is found, and the variant readings which occur in each make it certain that the Egyptian scribes had difficulty in understanding what they were writing. It may be said that this version of the cosmogony is incomplete, because it does not account for the origin of any of the gods except those who belong to the cycle of Osiris, and this objection is a valid one; but in this place we are only concerned to shew that Rā, the Sun-god, was evolved from the primeval abyss of water by the agency of the god Khepera, who brought this result about by pronouncing his own name. The great cosmic gods, such as Ptah and Khnemu, of whom mention will be made later, are the offspring of another set of religious views, and the cosmogony in which these play the leading parts is entirely different. We must notice, in passing, that the god whose words we have quoted above declares that he evolved himself under the form of Khepera, and that his name is Osiris, "the primeval matter of primeval matter," and that, as a result, Osiris is identical with Khepera in respect of his evolutions

[1] About B C. 300.

and new births. The word rendered "evolutions" is *kheperu*, literally "rollings"; and that rendered "primeval matter" is *paut*, the original "stuff" out of which everything was made. In both versions we are told that men and women came into being from the tears which fell from the "Eye" of Khepera, that is to say from the Sun, which, the god says, "I made take to up its place in my face, and afterwards it ruled the whole earth."

We have seen how Rā has become the visible type and symbol of God, and the creator of the world and of all that is therein; we may now consider the position which he held with respect to the dead. As far back as the period of the IVth dynasty, about B.C. 3700, he was regarded as the great god of heaven, and the king of all the gods, and divine beings, and of the beatified dead who dwelt therein. The position of the beatified in heaven is decided by Rā, and of all the gods there Osiris only appears to have the power to claim protection for his followers; the offerings which the deceased would make to Rā are actually presented to him by Osiris. At one time the Egyptian's greatest hope seems to have been that he might not only become "God, the son of God," by adoption, but that Rā would become actually his father. For in the text of Pepi I.,[1] it is said: "Pepi is the son of Rā who loveth him; and he goeth forth and raiseth himself

[1] Ed. Maspero, line 576.

up to heaven. Rā hath begotten Pepi, and he goeth forth and raiseth himself up to heaven. Rā hath conceived Pepi, and he goeth forth and raiseth himself up to heaven. Rā hath given birth to Pepi, and he goeth forth and raiseth himself up to heaven." Substantially these ideas remained the same from the earliest to the latest times, and Rā maintained his position as the great head of the companies, notwithstanding the rise of Amen into prominence, and the attempt to make Aten the dominant god of Egypt by the so-called "Disk worshippers." The following good typical examples of Hymns to Rā are taken from the oldest copies of the Theban Recension of the Book of the Dead.

I. From the Papyrus of Ani.[1]

"Homage to thee, O thou who hast come as Khepera, Khepera the creator of the gods. Thou risest and thou shinest, and thou makest light to be in thy mother Nut (*i.e.*, the sky); thou art crowned king of the gods. Thy mother Nut doeth an act of homage unto thee with both her hands. The land of Manu (*i.e.*, the land where the sun sets) receiveth thee with satisfaction, and the goddess Maāt embraceth thee both at morn and at eve.[2] Hail, all ye gods of the

---

[1] See *The Chapters of Coming Forth by Day*, p. 3.

[2] *I.e.*, Maāt, the goddess of law, order, regularity, and the like, maketh the sun to rise each day in his appointed place and at his appointed time with absolute and unfailing regularity.

HYMN TO RĀ (ABOUT B.C. 1550).

Temple of the Soul,[1] who weigh heaven and earth in the balance, and who provide divine food in abundance! Hail, Tatunen, thou One, thou Creator of mankind and Maker of the substance of the gods of the south and of the north, of the west and of the east! O come ye and acclaim Rā, the lord of heaven and the Creator of the gods, and adore ye him in his beautiful form as he cometh in the morning in his divine bark.

"O Rā, those who dwell in the heights and those who dwell in the depths adore thee. The god Thoth and the goddess Maāt have marked out for thee [thy course] for each and every day. <u>Thine enemy the Serpent hath been given over to the fire, the serpent-fiend Sebau hath fallen down headlong; his arms have been bound in chains, and thou hast hacked off his legs; and the sons of impotent revolt shall nevermore rise up against thee.</u> The Temple of the Aged One [2] (*i.e.*, Rā) keepeth festival, and the voice of those who rejoice is in the mighty dwelling. The gods exult when they see thy rising, O Rā, and when thy beams flood the world with light. The Majesty of the holy god goeth forth and advanceth even unto the land of Manu; he maketh brilliant the earth at his birth each day; he journeyeth on to the place where he was yesterday."

[1] *I.e.*, the soul referred to above in the account of the creation; see p. 24.
[2] *I.e*, Rā of Heliopolis.

II. From the Papyrus of Hunefer.[1]

"Homage to thee, O thou who art Rā when thou risest and Temu when thou settest. Thou risest, thou risest, thou shinest, thou shinest, O thou who art crowned king of the gods. Thou art the lord of heaven, thou art the lord of earth; thou art the creator of those who dwell in the heights, and of those who dwell in the depths. Thou art the One God who came into being in the beginning of time. Thou didst create the earth, thou didst fashion man, thou didst make the watery abyss of the sky, thou didst form Hāpi (*i.e.*, the Nile), thou didst create the great deep, and thou dost give life unto all that therein is. Thou hast knit together the mountains, thou hast made mankind and the beasts of the field to come into being, thou hast made the heavens and the earth. Worshipped be thou whom the goddess Maāt embraceth at morn and at eve. Thou dost travel across the sky with thy heart swelling with joy; the great deep of heaven is content thereat. The serpent-fiend Nak[2] hath fallen, and his arms are cut off. The Sektet[3] boat receiveth fair winds, and the heart of him that is in the shrine thereof rejoiceth.

"Thou art crowned Prince of heaven, and thou art

---

[1] From the Papyrus of Hunefer (Brit. Mus. No. 9901).
[2] A name of the serpent of darkness which Rā slew daily.
[3] The boat in which Rā sailed from noon to sunset.

the One [dowered with all sovereignty] who appearest in the sky. Rā is he who is true of voice.[1] Hail, thou divine youth, thou heir of everlastingness, thou self-begotten One! Hail, thou who didst give thyself birth! Hail, One, thou mighty being, of myriad forms and aspects, thou king of the world, prince of Annu (Heliopolis), lord of eternity, and ruler of everlastingness! The company of the gods rejoice when thou risest and dost sail across the sky, O thou who art exalted in the Sektet boat."

"Homage to thee, O Amen-Rā,[2] who dost rest upon Maāt;[3] thou passest over heaven and every face seeth thee. Thou dost wax great as thy Majesty doth advance, and thy rays are upon all faces. Thou art unknown, and no tongue can declare thy likeness; thou thyself alone [canst do this]. Thou art One . . . Men praise thee in thy name, and they swear by thee, for thou art lord over them. Thou hearest with thine ears, and thou seest with thine eyes. Millions of years have gone over the world. I cannot tell the number of those through which thou hast passed. Thy heart hath decreed a day of happiness in thy name of 'Traveller.' Thou dost pass over and dost travel through untold spaces [requiring] millions and hundreds

---

[1] *I.e.*, whatsoever Rā commandeth taketh place straightway; see the Chapter on the Judgment of the Dead, p. 110.

[2] On the god Amen, see the chapter, "The Gods of the Egyptians."

[3] *I.e.*, "thy existence, and thy risings and settings are ordered and defined by fixed, unchanging, and unalterable 'aw."

of thousands of years [to pass over]; thou passest through them in peace, and thou steerest thy way across the watery abyss to the place which thou lovest; this thou doest in one little moment of time, and then thou dost sink down and dost make an end of the hours."

III. From the Papyrus of Ani.[1]

The following beautiful composition, part hymn and part prayer, is of exceptional interest.

"Hail, thou Disk, thou lord of rays, who risest on the horizon day by day! Shine thou with thy beams of light upon the face of Osiris Ani, who is true of voice; for he singeth hymns of praise unto thee at dawn, and he maketh thee to set at eventide with words of adoration. May the soul of Ani come forth with thee into heaven, may he go forth in the Mātet boat. May he come into port in the Sektet boat, and may he cleave his path among the never-resting stars in the heavens.

"Osiris Ani, being in peace and triumph, adoreth his lord, the lord of eternity, saying, 'Homage to thee, O Heru-khuti (Harmachis), who art the god Khepera, the self-created one; when thou risest on the horizon and sheddest thy beams of light upon the lands of the North and of the South, thou art

[1] Plate 20.

beautiful, yea beautiful, and all the gods rejoice when they behold thee, the king of heaven. The goddess Nebt-Unnut is stablished upon thy head; and her uraei of the South and of the North are upon thy brow; she taketh up her place before thee. The god Thoth is stablished in the bows of thy boat to destroy utterly all thy foes. Those who are in the Tuat (underworld) come forth to meet thee, and they bow low in homage as they come towards thee, to behold thy beautiful form. And I have come before thee that I may be with thee to behold thy Disk each day. May I not be shut up [in the tomb], may I not be turned back, may the limbs of my body be made new again when I view thy beauties, even as [are those of] all thy favoured ones, because I am one of those who worshipped thee upon earth. May I come unto the land of eternity, may I come even unto the everlasting land, for behold, O my lord, this hast thou ordained for me.'

"'Homage to thee, O thou who risest in thy horizon as Rā, thou restest upon Maāt.[1] Thou passest over the sky, and every face watcheth thee and thy course, for thou hast been hidden from their gaze. Thou dost show thyself at dawn and at eventide day by day. The Sektet boat, wherein is thy Majesty, goeth forth with might; thy beams are upon [all] faces; thy rays of red and yellow cannot be known, and thy

[1] *I.e.*, unchanging and unalterable law.

bright beams cannot be told. The lands of the gods and the eastern lands of Punt[1] must be seen ere that which is hidden [in thee] may be measured.[2] Alone and by thyself thou dost manifest thyself [when] thou comest into being above Nu. May I advance, even as thou dost advance; may I never cease [to go forward], even as thy Majesty ceaseth not [to go forward], even though it be for a moment; for with strides dost thou in one brief moment pass over spaces which [man] would need hundreds of thousands, yea, millions of years to pass over; [this] thou doest, and then thon dost sink to rest. Thou puttest an end to the hours of the night, and thou dost count them, even thou; thou endest them in thine own appointed season, and the earth becometh light. Thou settest thyself before thy handiwork in the likeness of Rā; thou risest in the horizon.'

"Osiris, the scribe Ani, declareth his praise of thee when thou shinest, and when thou risest at dawn he crieth in his joy at thy birth, saying:—

"'Thou art crowned with the majesty of thy beauties; thou mouldest thy limbs as thou dost advance, and thou bringest them forth without birth-pangs in the form of Rā, as thou dost rise up in the celestial height. Grant thou that I may come unto the heaven which

---

[1] *I.e.*, the east and west coasts of the Red Sea, and the north-east coast of Africa.

[2] I am doubtful about the meaning of this passage.

is everlasting, and unto the mountain where dwell thy favoured ones. May I be joined unto those shining beings, holy and perfect, who are in the underworld; and may I come forth with them to behold thy beauties when thou shinest at eventide, and goest to thy mother Nut. Thou dost place thyself in the west, and my hands adore [thee] when thou settest as a living being.[1] Behold, thou art the everlasting creator, and thou art adored [as such when] thou settest in the heavens. I have given my heart to thee without wavering, O thou who art mightier than the gods.'

"A hymn of praise to thee, O thou who risest like unto gold, and who dost flood the world with light on the day of thy birth. Thy mother giveth thee birth, and straightway thou dost give light upon the path of [thy] Disk, O thou great Light who shinest in the heavens. Thou makest the generations of men to flourish through the Nile-flood, and thou dost cause gladness to exist in all lands, and in all cities, and in all temples. Thou art glorious by reason of thy splendours, and thou makest strong thy KA (*i.e.* Double) with divine foods, O thou mighty one of victories, thou Power of Powers, who dost make strong thy throne against evil fiends—thou who art glorious in Majesty in the Sektet boat, and most mighty in the Ātet[2] boat!"

[1] *I.e.*, "because when thou settest thou dost not die."
[2] The Sun's evening and morning boats respectively.

HYMN TO RĀ (ABOUT B.C. 1100). 37

This selection may be fittingly closed by a short hymn[1] which, though of a later date, reproduces in a brief form all the essentials of the longer hymns of the XVIIIth dynasty (about B.C. 1700 to 1400).

"Homage to thee, O thou glorious Being, thou who art dowered [with all sovereignty]. O Temu-Harmachis,[2] when thou risest in the horizon of heaven, a cry of joy cometh forth to thee from the mouth of all peoples. O thou beautiful Being, thou dost renew thyself in thy season in the form of the Disk within thy mother Hathor;[3] therefore in every place every heart swelleth with joy at thy rising for ever. The regions of the North and South come to thee with homage, and send forth acclamations at thy rising in the horizon of heaven; thou illuminest the two lands with rays of turquoise light. Hail, Rā, thou who art Rā-Harmachis, thou divine man-child, heir of eternity, self-begotten and self-born, king of the earth, prince of the underworld, governor of the regions of Ankert (*i.e.*, the underworld)! Thou didst come forth from the water, thou hast sprung from the god Nu, who cherisheth thee and ordereth thy members. Hail, god of life, thou lord of love, all men live when thou shinest; thou art crowned king of the gods. The goddess Nut doeth homage unto thee, and the goddess

---
[1] From the Papyrus of Nekht (Brit. Mus. No. 10,471).
[2] The evening and morning sun respectively.
[3] Like Nut, a goddess of the sky, but particularly of that portion of it in which the sun rises.

Maāt embraceth thee at all times. Those who are in thy following sing unto thee with joy and bow down their foreheads to the earth when they meet thee, thou lord of heaven, thou lord of earth, thou king of Right and Truth, thou lord of eternity, thou prince of everlastingness, thou sovereign of all the gods, thou god of life, thou creator of eternity, thou maker of heaven, wherein thou art firmly established. The company of the gods rejoice at thy rising, the earth is glad when it beholdeth thy rays; the peoples that have been long dead come forth with cries of joy to see thy beauties every day. Thou goest forth each day over heaven and earth, and art made strong each day by thy mother Nut. Thou passest through the heights of heaven, thy heart swelleth with joy; the abyss of the sky is content thereat. The Serpent-fiend hath fallen, his arms are hewn off, and the knife hath cut asunder his joints. Rā liveth in Maāt the beautiful. The Sektet boat draweth on and cometh into port; the South and the North, the West and the East, turn to praise thee, O thou primeval substance of the earth who didst come into being of thine own accord. Isis and Nephthys salute thee, they sing unto thee songs of joy at thy rising in the boat, they protect thee with their hands. The souls of the East follow thee, the souls of the West praise thee. Thou art the ruler of all the gods, and thou hast joy of heart within thy shrine; for the Serpent-fiend Nak hath been condemned to the fire, and thy heart shall be joyful for ever."

From the considerations set forth in the preceding pages, and from the extracts from religious texts of various periods, and from the hymns quoted, the reader may himself judge the views which the ancient Egyptian held concerning God Almighty and his visible type and symbol Rā, the Sun-god. Egyptologists differ in their interpretations of certain passages, but agree as to general facts. In dealing with the facts it cannot be too clearly understood that the religious ideas of the prehistoric Egyptian were very different from those of the cultured priest of Memphis in the IInd dynasty, or those of the worshippers of Temu or Atum, the god of the setting sun, in the IVth dynasty. The editors of religious texts of all periods have retained many grossly superstitious and coarse beliefs, which they knew well to be the products of the imaginations of their savage, or semi-savage ancestors, not because they themselves believed in them, or thought that the laity to whom they ministered would accept them, but because of their reverence for inherited traditions. The followers of every great religion in the world have never wholly shaken off all the superstitions which they have in all generations inherited from their ancestors; and what is true of the peoples of the past is true, in a degree, of the peoples of to-day. In the East the older the ideas, and beliefs, and traditions are, the more sacred they become; but this has not prevented men there from developing high moral and spiritual conceptions and continuing to believe in them, and among such must be counted the One, self-begotten, and self-existent God whom the Egyptians worshipped.

CHAPTER II.

OSIRIS THE GOD OF THE RESURRECTION.

THE Egyptians of every period in which they are known to us believed that Osiris was of divine origin, that he suffered death and mutilation at the hands of the powers of evil, that after a great struggle with these powers he rose again, that he became henceforth the king of the underworld and judge of the dead, and that because he had conquered death the righteous also might conquer death; and they raised Osiris to such an exalted position in heaven that he became the equal and, in certain cases, the superior of Rā, the Sun-god, and ascribed to him the attributes which belong unto God. However far back we go, we find that these views about Osiris are assumed to be known to the reader of religious texts and accepted by him, and in the earliest funeral book the position of Osiris in respect of the other gods is identical with that which he is made to hold in the latest copies of the Book of the Dead. The first writers of the ancient hieroglyphic funeral texts and their later editors have assumed so completely that the history of Osiris was known unto all men, that none of them, as far as we know, thought it necessary to write down a connected narrative of the life and sufferings upon earth of this god, or if they did, it has not come down to us. Even in the Vth dynasty we find Osiris and the gods of his cycle, or company, occupying a peculiar and special place in the compositions written for the benefit of the dead, and the stone and other monuments which belong to still earlier periods mention ceremonies the performance of which assumed the substantial accuracy of the history of Osiris as made known to us by later writers. But we have a connected history of Osiris which, though not written in Egyptian, contains so much that is of Egyptian origin that we may be sure that its author drew his information from Egyptian sources: I refer to the work, *De Iside et Osiride*, of the Greek writer, Plutarch, who flourished about the middle of the first century of our era. In it, unfortunately, Plutarch identifies certain of the Egyptian gods with the gods of the Greeks, and he adds a number of statements which rest either upon his own imagination, or are the results of misinformation. The translation [1] by Squire runs as follows:—

"Rhea,[2] say they, having accompanied Saturn [3] by

---

[1] *Plutarchi de Iside et Osiride liber: Græce et Anglice.* By S. Squire, Cambridge, 1744.

[2] *I.e.*, Nut.   [3] *I.e.*, Seb.

THE BIRTH OF OSIRIS. 43

stealth, was discovered by the Sun,[1] who hereupon denounced a curse upon her, 'that she should not be delivered in any month or year'—Mercury, however, being likewise in love with the same goddess, in recompense of the favours which he had received from her, plays at tables with the Moon, and wins from her the seventieth part of each of her illuminations; these several parts, making in the whole five days, he afterwards joined together, and added to the three hundred and sixty, of which the year formerly consisted, which days therefore are even yet called by the Egyptians the Epact or superadded, and observed by them as the birthdays of their gods. For upon the first of them, say they, was OSIRIS born, just at whose entrance into the world a voice was heard, saying, 'The lord of all the earth is born.' There are some indeed who relate this circumstance in a different manner, as that a certain person, named Pamyles, as he was fetching water from the temple of Jupiter at Thebes, heard a voice commanding him to proclaim aloud that 'the good and great king Osiris was then born'; and that for this reason Saturn committed the education of the child to him, and that in memory of this event the Pamylia were afterwards instituted, a festival much resembling the Phalliphoria or Priapeia of the Greeks. Upon the second of these days was AROUERIS [2] born, whom some call Apollo, and others distinguish by the

---

[1] *I.e.*, Râ.   [2] *Ie*, Heru-ur, "Horus the Elder."

name of the elder Orus. Upon the third Typho[1] came into the world, being born neither at the proper time, nor by the proper place, but forcing his way through a wound which he had made in his mother's side. ISIS was born upon the fourth of them in the marshes of Egypt, as NEPTHYS was upon the last, whom some call Teleute and Aphrodite, and others Nike—Now as to the fathers of these children, the two first of them are said to have been begotten by the Sun, Isis by Mercury, Typho and Nepthys by Saturn; and accordingly, the third of these superadded days, because it was looked upon as the birthday of Typho, was regarded by the kings as inauspicious, and consequently they neither transacted any business on it, or even suffered themselves to take any refreshment until the evening. They further add, that Typho married Nepthys; and that Isis and Osiris, having a mutual affection, loved each other in their mother's womb before they were born, and that from this commerce sprang Aroueris, whom the Egyptians likewise call the elder Orus, and the Greeks Apollo.

"Osiris, being now become king of Egypt, applied himself towards civilizing his countrymen, by turning them from their former indigent and barbarous course of life; he moreover taught them how to cultivate and improve the fruits of the earth; he gave them a body of laws to regulate their conduct by, and instructed

---

[1] *I.e.*, Set.

them in that reverence and worship which they were to pay to the gods. With the same good disposition he afterwards travelled over the rest of the world inducing the people everywhere to submit to his discipline; not indeed compelling them by force of arms, but persuading them to yield to the strength of his reasons, which were conveyed to them in the most agreeable manner, in hymns and songs, accompanied by instruments of music: from which last circumstance the Greeks conclude him to have been the same with their Dionysius or Bacchus—During Osiris' absence from his kingdom, Typho had no opportunity of making any innovations in the state, Isis being extremely vigilant in the government, and always upon her guard. After his return, however, having first persuaded seventy-two other persons to join with him in the conspiracy, together with a certain queen of Ethiopia named Aso, who chanced to be in Egypt at that time, he contrived a proper stratagem to execute his base designs. For having privily taken the measure of Osiris' body, he caused a chest to be made exactly of the same size with it, as beautiful as may be, and set off with all the ornaments of art. This chest he brought into his banqueting-room; where, after it had been much admired by all who were present, Typho, as it were in jest, promised to give it to any one of them whose body upon trial it might be found to fit. Upon this the whole company,

OSIRIS IS TREACHEROUSLY MURDERED.

one after another, go into it; but as it did not fit any of them, last of all Osiris lays himself down in it, upon which the conspirators immediately ran together, clapped the cover upon it, and then fastened it down on the outside with nails, pouring likewise melted lead over it. After this they carried it away to the river side, and conveyed it to the sea by the Tanaïtic mouth of the Nile; which, for this reason, is still held in the utmost abomination by the Egyptians, and never named by them but with proper marks of detestation. These things, say they, were thus executed upon the 17th[1] day of the month Athyr, when the sun was in Scorpio, in the 28th year of Osiris' reign; though there are others who tell us that he was no more than 28 years old at this time.

"The first who knew the accident which had befallen their king were the Pans and Satyrs who inhabited the country about Chemmis (Panopolis); and they immediately acquainting the people with the news gave the first occasion to the name Panic Terrors, which has ever since been made use of to signify any sudden affright or amazement of a multitude. As to Isis, as soon as the report reached her she immediately cut off one of the locks of her hair,[2] and put on mourning apparel upon the very spot where she then happened to be, which accordingly from this accident

[1] In the Egyptian calendar this day was marked triply unlucky.
[2] The hair cut off as a sign of mourning was usually laid in the tomb of the dead.

has ever since been called Koptis, or *the city of mourning*, though some are of opinion that this word rather signifies *deprivation*. After this she wandered everywhere about the country full of disquietude and perplexity in search of the chest, inquiring of every person she met with, even of some children whom she chanced to see, whether they knew what was become of it. Now it happened that these children had seen what Typho's accomplices had done with the body, and accordingly acquainted her by what mouth of the Nile it had been conveyed into the sea—For this reason therefore the Egyptians look upon children as endued with a kind of faculty of divining, and in consequence of this notion are very curious in observing the accidental prattle which they have with one another whilst they are at play (especially if it be in a sacred place), forming omens and presages from it—Isis, during this interval, having been informed that Osiris, deceived by her sister Nepthys who was in love with him, had unwittingly united with her instead of herself, as she concluded from the melilot-garland,[5] which he had left with her, made it her business likewise to search out the child, the fruit of this unlawful commerce (for her sister, dreading the anger of her husband Typho, had exposed it as soon as it was born), and accordingly, after much pains and difficulty, by means of some dogs that conducted her to the place

[5] *I.e.*, a wreath of clover.

where it was, she found it and bred it up; so that in process of time it became her constant guard and attendant, and from hence obtained the name of Anubis, being thought to watch and guard the gods, as dogs do mankind.

"At length she receives more particular news of the chest, that it had been carried by the waves of the sea to the coast of Byblos,[1] and there gently lodged in the branches of a bush of Tamarisk, which, in a short time, had shot up into a large and beautiful tree, growing round the chest and enclosing it on every side, so that it was not to be seen; and farther, that the king of the country, amazed at its unusual size, had cut the tree down, and made that part of the trunk wherein the chest was concealed, a pillar to support the roof of his house. These things, say they, being made known to Isis in an extraordinary manner by the report of Demons, she immediately went to Byblos; where, setting herself down by the side of a fountain, she refused to speak to anybody, excepting only to the queen's women who chanced to be there; these indeed she saluted and caressed in the kindest manner possible, plaiting their hair for them, and transmitting into them part of that wonderfully grateful odour which issued from her own body. This raised a great desire in the queen their mistress to see the stranger who had this

---

[1] Not the Byblos of Syria (Jebêl) but the papyrus swamps of the Delta.

ISIS TRANSFORMS HERSELF.

admirable faculty of transfusing so fragrant a smell from herself into the hair and skin of other people. She therefore sent for her to court, and, after a further acquaintance with her, made her nurse to one of her sons. Now the name of the king who reigned at this time at Byblos, was Melcarthus, as that of his queen was Astarte, or, according to others, Saosis, though some call her Nemanoun, which answers to the Greek name Athenais.

"Isis fed the child by giving it her finger to suck instead of the breast; she likewise put him every night into the fire in order to consume his mortal part, whilst transforming herself into a swallow, she hovered round the pillar and bemoaned her sad fate. Thus continued she to do for some time, till the queen, who stood watching her, observing the child to be all in a flame, cryed out, and thereby deprived him of that immortality which would otherwise have been conferred upon him. The Goddess upon this, discovering herself, requested that the pillar, which supported the roof, might be given her; which she accordingly took down, and then easily cutting it open, after she had taken out what she wanted, she wrapped up the remainder of the trunk in fine linnen, and pouring perfumed oil upon it, delivered it again into the hands of the king and queen (which piece of wood is to this day preserved in the temple of Isis, and worshipped by the people of Byblos). When this was done, she threw herself upon the chest, making at the same time such a loud and terrible lamentation over it, as frightened the younger of the king's sons, who heard her, out of his life. But the elder of them she took with her and set sail with the chest for Egypt; and it being now about morning, the river Phædrus sending forth a rough and sharp air, she in her anger dried up its current.

"No sooner was she arrived at a desart place, where she imagined herself to be alone, but she presently opened the chest, and laying her face upon her dead husband's, embraced his corpse, and wept bitterly; but perceiving that the little boy had silently stolen behind her, and found out the occasion of her grief, she turned herself about on the sudden, and in her anger gave him so fierce and stern a look that he immediately died of the affright. Others indeed say that his death did not happen in this manner, but, as was hinted above, that he fell into the sea, and afterwards received the greatest honours on account of the Goddess; for that the Maneros,[1] whom the Egyptians so frequently call upon in their banquets, is none other than this very boy. This relation is again contradicted by such as tell us that the true name of the child was Palæstinus, or Pelusius, and that the city of this name was built by the Goddess in memory of

---

[1] A son of the first Egyptian king, who died in his early youth; see Herodotus, ii. 79.

him; adding farther, that the Maneros above mentioned is thus honoured by the Egyptians at their feasts, because he was the first who invented music. There are others, again, who affirm that Maneros is not the name of any particular person, but a mere customary form, and complimental manner of greeting made use of by the Egyptians one towards another at their more solemn feasts and banquets, meaning no more by it, than to wish, that what they were then about might prove fortunate and happy to them, for that this is the true import of the word. In like manner, say they, the human skeleton, which at these times of jollity is carried about in a box, and shewn to all the guests, is not designed, as some imagine, to represent the particular misfortunes of Osiris, but rather to remind them of their mortality, and thereby to excite them freely to make use of and to enjoy the good things which are set before them, seeing they must quickly become such as they there saw; and that this is the true reason of introducing it at their banquets—but to proceed in the narration.

"Isis intending a visit to her son Orus, who was brought up at Butus, deposited the chest in the meanwhile in a remote and unfrequented place: Typho however, as he was one night hunting by the light of the moon, accidentally met with it; and knowing the body which was enclosed in it, tore it into several pieces, fourteen in all, dispersing them up and down in different parts of the country—Upon being made acquainted with this event, Isis once more sets out in search of the scattered fragments of her husband's body, making use of a boat made of the reed Papyrus in order the more easily to pass thro' the lower and fenny parts of the country—For which reason, say they, the crocodile never touches any persons, who sail in this sort of vessels, as either fearing the anger of the goddess, or else respecting it on account of its having once carried her. To this occasion therefore is it to be imputed, that there are so many different sepulchres of Osiris shewn in Egypt; for we are told, that wherever Isis met with any of the scattered limbs of her husband, she there buried it. There are others however who contradict this relation, and tell us, that this variety of Sepulchres was owing rather to the policy of the queen, who, instead of the real body, as was pretended, presented these several cities with the image only of her husband: and that she did this, not only to render the honours, which would by this means be paid to his memory, more extensive, but likewise that she might hereby elude the malicious search of Typho; who, if he got the better of Orus in the war wherein they were going to be engaged, distracted by this multiplicity of Sepulchres, might despair of being able to find the true one—we are told moreover, that notwithstanding all her search, Isis was never able to recover the member of Osiris, which having been thrown into the Nile immediately upon its separation from the rest of the body, had been devoured by the Lepidotus, the Phagrus, and the Oxyrynchus, fish which of all others, for this reason, the Egyptians have in more especial avoidance. In order however to make some amends for the loss, Isis consecrated the Phallus made in imitation of it, and instituted a solemn festival to its memory, which is even to this day observed by the Egyptians.

"After these things, Osiris returning from the other world, appeared to his son Orus, encouraged him to the battle, and at the same time instructed him in the exercise of arms. He then asked him, 'what he thought was the most glorious action a man could perform?' to which Orus replied, 'to revenge the injuries offered to his father and mother.' He then asked him, 'what animal he thought most serviceable to a soldier?' and being answered 'a horse'; this raised the wonder of Osiris, so that he farther questioned him, 'why he preferred a horse before a lion?' because, adds Orus, 'tho' the lion be the more serviceable creature to one who stands in need of help, yet is the horse[1] more useful in overtaking and cutting off a flying adversary.' These replies much rejoiced Osiris, as they showed him that his son was

---

[1] The horse does not appear to have been known in Egypt before the XVIIIth dynasty; this portion of Plutarch's version of the history of Osiris must, then, be later than B.C. 1500.

sufficiently prepared for his enemy—We are moreover told, that among the great numbers who were continually deserting from Typho's party was his concubine Thueris, and that a serpent pursuing her as she was coming over to Orus, was slain by her soldiers—the memory of which action, say they, is still preserved in that cord which is thrown into the midst of their assemblies, and then chopt into pieces—Afterwards it came to a battle between them which lasted many days; but victory at length inclined to Orus, Typho himself being taken prisoner. Isis however, to whose custody he was committed, was so far from putting him to death, that she even loosed his bonds and set him at liberty. This action of his mother so extremely incensed Orus, that he laid hands upon her, and pulled off the ensign of royalty which she wore on her head; and instead thereof Hermes clapt on an helmet made in the shape of an oxe's head—After this, Typho publicly accused Orus of bastardy; but by the assistance of Hermes (Thoth) his legitimacy was fully established by the judgment of the Gods themselves—After this, there were two other battles fought between them, in both of which Typho had the worst. Furthermore, Isis is said to have accompanied with Osiris after his death, and in consequence hereof to have brought forth Harpocrates, who came into the world before his time, and lame in his lower limbs."

When we examine this story by the light of the

results of hieroglyphic decipherment, we find that a large portion of it is substantiated by Egyptian texts: *e.g.*, Osiris was the son of Seb and Nut; the Epact is known in the Calendars as "the five additional days of the year"; the five gods, Osiris, Horus, Set, Isis, and Nephthys, were born on the days mentioned by Plutarch; the 17th day of Athyr (Hathor) is marked as triply unlucky in the Calendars; the wanderings and troubles of Isis are described, and "lamentations" which she is supposed to have uttered are found in the texts; lists of the shrines of Osiris are preserved in several inscriptions; the avenging of his father by Horus is referred to frequently in papyri and other documents; the conflict between Set and Horus is described fully in a papyrus in the British Museum (No. 10,184); a hymn in the papyrus of Hunefer relates all that Thoth performed for Osiris; and the begetting of Horus by Osiris after death is mentioned in a hymn to Osiris dating from the XVIIIth dynasty in the following passage :—

"Thy sister put forth her protecting power for thee, she scattered abroad those who were her enemies, she drove away evil hap, she pronounced mighty words of power, she made cunning her tongue, and her words failed not. The glorious Isis was perfect in command and in speech, and she avenged her brother. She sought him without ceasing, she wandered round and round the earth uttering cries of pain, and she rested (*or* alighted) not until she had found him. She overshadowed him with her feathers, she made air (*or* wind) with her wings, and she uttered cries at the burial of her brother. She raised up the prostrate form of him whose heart was still, she took from him of his essence, she conceived and brought forth a child, she suckled it in secret, and none knew the place thereof; and the arm of the child hath waxed strong in the great house of Seb. The company of the gods rejoice, and are glad at the coming of Osiris's son Horus, and firm of heart and triumphant is the son of Isis, 'the heir of Osiris." [1]

What form the details of the history of Osiris took in the early dynasties it is impossible to say, and we know not whether Osiris was the god of the resurrection to the predynastic or prehistoric Egyptians, or whether that *rôle* was attributed to him after Mena began to rule in Egypt. There is, however, good reason for assuming that in the earliest dynastic times he occupied the position of god and judge of those who had risen from the dead by his help, for already in the IVth dynasty, about B.C. 3800, king Men-kau-Rā (the Mycerinus of the Greeks) is identified with him, and on his coffin not only is he called "Osiris, King of the South and North, Men-kau-Rā, living for ever," but the genealogy of Osiris is attributed to him, and

---

[1] This remarkable hymn was first made known by Chabas, who published a translation of it, with notes, in *Revue Archéologique*, Paris, 1857, t. xiv. p. 65 ff.

1. Isis suckling her child Horus in the papyrus swamps.
2. Thoth giving the emblem of magical protection to Isis.
3. Amen-Rā presenting the symbol of "life" to Isis.

4. The goddess Nekhebet presenting years, and life, stability, power, and sovereignty to the son of Osiris.
5. The goddess Sati presenting periods of years, and life, stability, power, and sovereignty to the son of Osiris.

OSIRIS THE GOD-MAN.

he is declared to be "born of heaven, offspring of Nut, flesh and bone of Seb." It is evident that the priests of Heliopolis "edited" the religious texts copied and multiplied in the College to suit their own views, but in the early times when they began their work, the worship of Osiris was so widespread, and the belief in him as the god of the resurrection so deeply ingrained in the hearts of the Egyptians, that even in the Heliopolitan system of theology Osiris and his cycle, or company of gods, were made to hold a very prominent position. He represented to men the idea of a man who was both god and man, and he typified to the Egyptians in all ages the being who by reason of his sufferings and death as a man could sympathize with them in their own sickness and death. The idea of his human personality also satisfied their cravings and yearnings for intercourse with a being who, though he was partly divine, yet had much in common with themselves. Originally they looked upon Osiris as a man who lived on the earth as they lived, who ate and drank, who suffered a cruel death, who by the help of certain gods triumphed over death, and attained unto everlasting life. But what Osiris did they could do, and what the gods did for Osiris they must also do for them, and as the gods brought about his resurrection so they must bring about theirs, and as they made him the ruler of the underworld so they must make them to enter his kingdom and to live there as long as the god himself lived. Osiris, in some of his aspects, was identified with the Nile, and with Rā, and with several other "gods" known to the Egyptians, but it was in his aspect as god of the resurrection and of eternal life that he appealed to men in the valley of the Nile; and for thousands of years men and women died believing that, inasmuch as all that was done for Osiris would be done for them symbolically, they like him would rise again and inherit life everlasting. However far back we trace religious ideas in Egypt, we never approach a time when it can be said that there did not exist a belief in the Resurrection, for everywhere it is assumed that Osiris rose from the dead; sceptics must have existed, and they probably asked their priests what the Corinthians asked Saint Paul, "How are the dead raised up? and with what body do they come?" But beyond doubt the belief in the Resurrection was accepted by the dominant classes in Egypt. The ceremonies which the Egyptians performed with the view of assisting the deceased to pass the ordeal of the judgment, and to overcome his enemies in the next world, will be described elsewhere, as also will be the form in which the dead were raised up; we therefore return to the theological history of Osiris.

The centre and home of the worship of Osiris in Egypt under the early dynasties was Abydos, where the head of the god was said to be buried. It spread north and south in the course of time, and several large cities claimed to possess one or other of the limbs of his body. The various episodes in the life of the god were made the subject of solemn representations in the temple, and little by little the performance of the obligatory and non-obligatory services in connection with them occupied, in certain temples, the greater part of the time of the priests. The original ideas concerning the god were forgotten and new ones grew up; from being the *example* of a man who had risen from the dead and had attained unto life everlasting, he became the *cause* of the resurrection of the dead; and the power to bestow eternal life upon mortals was transferred from the gods to him. The alleged dismemberment of Osiris was forgotten in the fact that he dwelt in a perfect body in the underworld, and that, whether dismembered or not, he had become after his death the father of Horus by Isis. As early as the XIIth dynasty, about B.C. 2500, the worship of this god had become almost universal, and a thousand years later Osiris had become a sort of national god. The attributes of the great cosmic gods were ascribed to him, and he appeared to man not only as the god and judge of the dead, but also as the creator of the world and of all things in it. He who was the son of Rā became the equal of his father, and he took his place side by side with him in heaven.

We have an interesting proof of the identification of Osiris with Rā in Chapter XVII. of the Book of the Dead. It will be remembered that this Chapter consists of a series of what might almost be called articles of faith, each of which is followed by one or more explanations which represent one or more quite different opinions; the Chapter also is accompanied by a series of Vignettes. In line 110 it is said, "I am the soul which dwelleth in the two *tchafi*.[1] What is this then? It is Osiris when he goeth into Tattu (*i.e.*, Busiris) and findeth there the soul of Rā; there the one god embraceth the other, and souls spring into being within the two *tchafi.*" In the Vignette which illustrates this passage the souls of Rā and Osiris are seen in the forms of hawks standing on a pylon and facing each other in Tattu; the former has upon his head a disk, and the latter, who is human-headed, the white crown. It is a noticeable fact that even at his meeting with Rā the soul of Osiris preserves the human face, the sign of his kinship with man.

Now Osiris became not only the equal of Rā, but, in many respects, a greater god than he. It is said that from the nostrils of the head of Osiris, which was buried at Abydos, came forth the scarabæus[2] which was at once the emblem and type of the god Khepera, who caused all things to come into being, and of the resurrection. In this manner Osiris became the source and origin of gods, men, and things, and

---

[1] *I.e.*, the souls of Osiris and Rā.
[2] See von Bergmann in *Aeg Zeitschrift*, 1880, p. 88 ff.

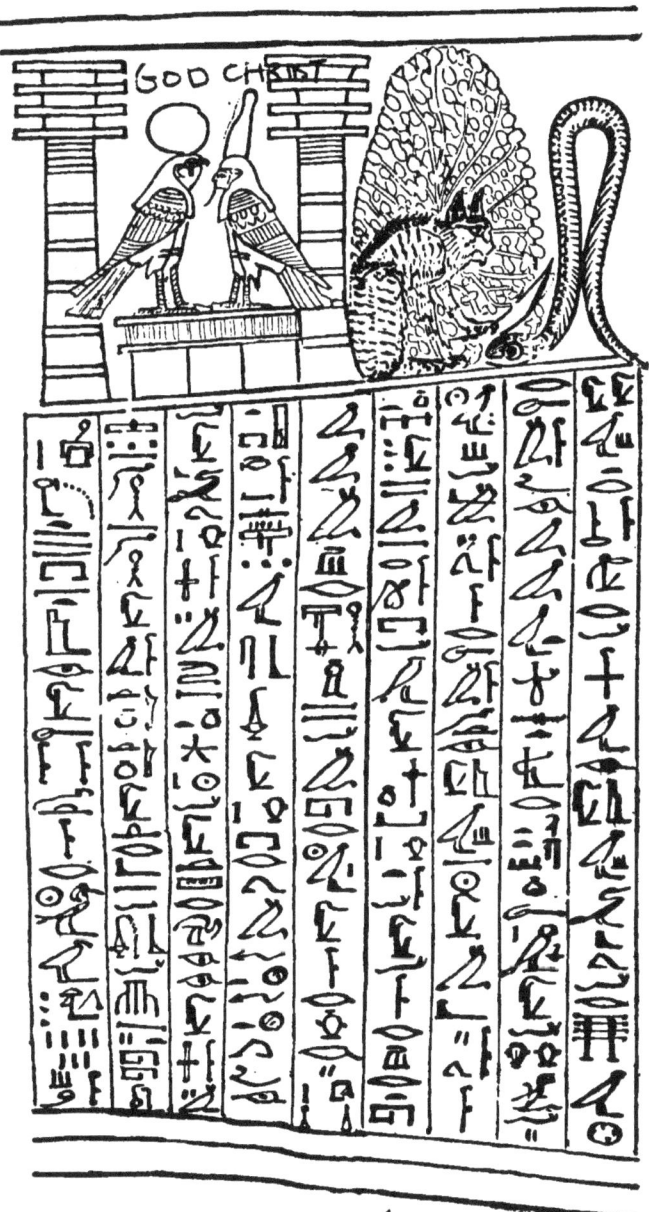

The soul of Rā (1) meeting the soul of Osiris (2) in Tattu. The cat (i.e., Rā) by the Persea tree (3) cutting off the head of the serpent which typified night.

HYMN TO OSIRIS.

the manhood of the god was forgotten. The next step was to ascribe to him the attributes of God, and in the XVIIIth and XIXth dynasties he seems to have disputed the sovereignty of the three companies of gods, that is to say of the trinity of trinities of trinities,[1] with Amen-Rā, who by this time was usually called the "king of the gods." The ideas held concerning Osiris at this period will best be judged by the following extracts from contemporary hymns:—

"Glory[2] be to thee, O Osiris, Un-nefer, the great god within Abtu (Abydos), king of eternity, lord of everlastingness, who passest through millions of years in thy existence. The eldest son of the womb of Nut, engendered by Seb the Ancestor [of the gods], lord of the crowns of the South and of the North, lord of the lofty white crown; as prince of gods and men he hath received the crook and the whip, and the dignity of his divine fathers. Let thy heart, which dwelleth in the mountain of Ament, be content, for thy son Horus is stablished upon thy throne. Thou art crowned lord of Tattu (Busiris) and ruler in Abydos."

"Praise[3] be unto thee, O Osiris, lord of eternity, Un-nefer, Heru-Khuti (Harmachis) whose forms are manifold, and whose attributes are great, who art Ptah-Seker-Tem in Annu (Heliopolis), the lord of the

---

[1] Each company of the gods contained three trinities or triads.
[2] See *Chapters of Coming Forth by Day* (translation), p. 11.
[3] *Ibid.*, p. 34.

hidden place, and the creator of Het-ka-Ptah (Memphis) and of the gods [therein], the guide of the underworld, whom [the gods] glorify when thou settest in Nut. Isis embraceth thee in peace, and she driveth away the fiends from the mouth of thy paths. Thou turnest thy face upon Amentet, and thou makest the earth to shine as with refined copper. The dead rise up to see thee, they breathe the air and they look upon thy face when the disk riseth on its horizon; their hearts are at peace, inasmuch as they behold thee, O thou who art eternity and everlastingness."

In the latter extract Osiris is identified with the great gods of Heliopolis and Memphis, where shrines of the Sun-god existed in almost pre-dynastic times, and finally is himself declared to be "eternity and everlastingness"; thus the ideas of resurrection and immortality are united in the same divine being. In the following Litany the process of identification with the gods is continued:—

1. "Homage to thee, O thou who art the starry deities in Annu, and the heavenly beings in Kher-âba;[1] thou god Unti,[2] who art more glorious than the gods who are hidden in Annu. O grant thou unto me a path whereon I may pass in peace, for I am just and true; I have not spoken lies wittingly, nor have I done aught with deceit."

[1] A district near Memphis.
[2] A god who walks belore the boat of the god Af, holding a star in each hand.

A LITANY. 67

2. "Homage to thee, O An in Antes, Harmachis; thou stridest over heaven with long strides, O Harmachis. O grant thou unto me a path," etc.[1]

3. "Homage to thee, O soul of everlastingness, thou Soul who dwellest in Tattu, Un-nefer, son of Nut; thou art lord of Akert (*i.e.*, the underworld). O grant thou unto me a path," etc.

4. "Homage to thee in thy dominion over Tattu; the Ureret crown is stablished upon thy head; thou art the One who maketh the strength which protecteth himself, and thou dwellest in peace in Tattu. O grant thou unto me a path," etc.

5. "Homage to thee, O lord of the Acacia [2] tree, the Seker boat [3] is set upon its sledge; thou turnest back the Fiend, the worker of Evil, and thou causest the Utchat (*i.e.*, the Eye of Horus or Rā), to rest upon its seat. O grant thou unto me a path," etc.

6. "Homage to thee, O thou who art mighty in thine hour, thou great and mighty Prince, dweller in An-rut-f,[4] lord of eternity and creator of everlastingness, thou art the lord of Suten-henen (*i.e.*, Heracleopolis Magna). O grant," etc.

7. "Homage to thee, O thou who restest upon

[1] This petition is only written once, but it is intended to be repeated after each of the nine sections of the Litany.
[2] This tree was in Heliopolis, and the Cat, *i.e*, the Sun, sat near it. (See p. 63).
[3] The ceremony of setting the Seker boat on its sledge was performed at dawn.
[4] The place where nothing grows—the underworld.

Right and Truth, thou art lord of Abydos, and thy limbs are joined unto Ta-tchesert (*i.e.*, the Holy Land, the underworld); thou art he to whom fraud and guile are hateful. O grant," etc.

8. "Homage to thee, O thou who art within thy boat, thou bringest Hāpi (*i.e.*, the Nile) forth from his source; the light shineth upon thy body, and thou art the dweller in Nekhen. O grant," etc.

9. "Homage to thee, O creator of the gods, thou king of the South and of the North, O Osiris, victorious one, ruler of the world in thy gracious seasons; thou art the lord of the celestial world. O grant," etc.

And, again: "Rā setteth as Osiris with all the diadems of the divine spirits and of the gods of Amentet. He is the one divine form, the hidden one of the Tuat, the holy Soul at the head of Amentet, Un-nefer, whose duration of life is for ever and ever."[1]

We have already referred to the help which Thoth gave to Isis when he provided her with the words which caused her dead husband to live again, but the best summary of the good deeds which this god wrought for Osiris is contained in a hymn in the *Papyrus of Hunefer*,[2] where the deceased is made to say:—

"I have come unto thee, O son of Nut, Osiris, Prince of everlastingness; I am in the following of the god Thoth, and I have rejoiced at everything which he

---

[1] See *Chapters of Coming Forth by Day*, p. 334. [2] *Ibid.*, p. 343.

hath done for thee. He brought the sweet air into thy nostrils, and life and strength to thy beautiful face; and the north wind which cometh forth from Temu for thy nostrils, O lord, of Ta-tchesert. He made the god Shu to shine upon thy body; he illumined thy path with rays of light; he destroyed for thee the faults and defects of thy members by the magical power of the words of his mouth; he made Set and Horus to be at peace for thy sake; he destroyed the storm-wind and the hurricane; he made the two combatants (*i.e.*, Set and Horus) to be gracious unto thee and the two lands to be at peace before thee; he did away the wrath which was in their hearts, and each became reconciled unto his brother (*i.e.*, thyself).

"Thy son Horus is triumphant in the presence of the full assembly of the gods, the sovereignty over the world hath been given unto him, and his dominion extendeth unto the uttermost parts of the earth. The throne of the god Seb hath been adjudged unto him, together with the rank which was created by the god Temu, and which hath been stablished by decrees [made] in the Chamber of Archives, and hath been inscribed upon an iron tablet according to the command of thy father Ptah-Tanen when he sat upon the great throne. He hath set his brother upon that which the god Shu beareth up (*i.e.*, the heavens), to stretch out the waters over the mountains, and to make to spring up that which groweth upon the hills, and the grain (?)

which shooteth upon the earth, and he giveth increase by water and by land. Gods celestial and gods terrestrial transfer themselves to the service of thy son Horus, and they follow him into his hall [where] a decree is passed that he shall be lord over them, and they do [his will] straightway.

"Let thy heart rejoice, O lord of the gods, let thy heart rejoice greatly; Egypt and the Red Land are at peace, and they serve humbly under thy sovereign power. The temples are stablished upon their own lands, cities and nomes possess securely the goods which they have in their names, and we will make unto thee the divine offerings which we are bound to make, and offer sacrifices in thy name for ever. Acclamations are made in thy name, libations are poured out to thy KA, and sepulchral meals [are brought unto thee] by the spirits who are in thy following, and water is sprinkled. . . . on each side of the souls of the dead in this land. Every plan for thee which hath been decreed by the commands of Rā from the beginning hath been perfected. Now therefore, O son of Nut, thou art crowned as Neb-er-tcher is crowned at his rising. Thou livest, thou art stablished, thou renewest thy youth, and thou art true and perfect; thy father Rā maketh strong thy members, and the company of the gods make acclamations unto thee. The goddess Isis is with thee and she never leaveth thee; [thou art] not overthrown by thine

OSIRIS AND THE SECOND BIRTH.

enemies. The lords of all lands praise thy beauties, even as they praise Rā when he riseth at the beginning of each day. Thou risest up like an exalted being upon thy standard, thy beauties lift up the face [of man] and make long [his] stride. The sovereignty of thy father Seb hath been given unto thee, and the goddess Nut, thy mother, who gave birth to the gods, brought thee forth as the firstborn of five gods, and created thy beauties and fashioned thy members. Thou art stablished as king, the white crown is upon thy head, and thou hast grasped in thy hands the crook and whip; whilst thou wert in the womb, and hadst not as yet come forth therefrom upon the earth, thou wert crowned lord of the two lands, and the 'Atef' crown of Rā was upon thy brow. The gods come unto thee bowing low to the ground, and they hold thee in fear; they retreat and depart when they see thee with the terror of Rā, and the victory of thy Majesty is in their hearts. Life is with thee, and offerings of meat and drink follow thee, and that which is thy due is offered up before thy face."

In one paragraph of another somewhat similar hymn[1] other aspects of Osiris are described, and after the words "Homage to thee, O Governor of those who are in Amentet," he is called the being who "giveth birth unto men and women a second time,"[2] *i.e.*, "who

---
[1] See *Chapters of Coming Forth by Day*, p. 342.
[2] The words are *mes temcmu em ars*.

maketh mortals to be born again." As the whole paragraph refers to Osiris "renewing himself," and to his making himself "young like unto Rā each and every day," there can be no doubt that the resurrection of the dead, that is to say, their birth into a new life, is what the writer means by the second birth of men and women. From this passage also we may see that Osiris has become the equal of Rā, and that he has passed from being the god of the dead to being the god of the living. Moreover, at the time when the above extracts were copied Osiris was not only assumed to have occupied the position which Rā formerly held, but his son Horus, who was begotten after his death, was, by virtue of his victory over Set, admitted to be the heir and successor of Osiris. And he not only succeeded to the "rank and dignity" of his father Osiris, but in his aspect of "avenger of his father," he gradually acquired the peculiar position of intermediary and intercessor on behalf of the children of men. Thus in the Judgment Scene he leads the deceased into the presence of Osiris and makes an appeal to his father that the deceased may be allowed to enjoy the benefits enjoyed by all those who are "true of voice" and justified in the judgment. Such an appeal, addressed to Osiris in the presence of Isis, from the son born under such remarkable circumstances was, the Egyptian thought, certain of acceptance; and the offspring of a father, after the death

PRAYER TO OSIRIS.

of whose body he was begotten, was naturally the best advocate for the deceased.

But although such exalted ideas of Osiris and his position among the gods obtained generally in Egypt during the XVIIIth dynasty (about B.C. 1600) there is evidence that some believed that in spite of every precaution the body might decay, and that it was necessary to make a special appeal unto Osiris if this dire result was to be avoided. The following remarkable prayer was first found inscribed upon a linen swathing which had enveloped the mummy of Thothmes III., but since that time the text, written in hieroglyphics, has been found inscribed upon the *Papyrus of Nu*,[1] and it is, of course, to be found also in the late papyrus preserved at Turin, which the late Dr. Lepsius published so far back as 1842. This text, which is now generally known as Chapter CLIV of the Book of the Dead, is entitled "The Chapter of not letting the body perish." The text begins:—

"Homage to thee, O my divine father Osiris! I have come to thee that thou mayest embalm, yea embalm these my members, for I would not perish and come to an end, [but would be] even like unto my divine father Khepera, the divine type of him that never saw corruption. Come, then, and make me to have the mastery over my breath, O thou lord

---

[1] Brit. Mus., No. 10,477, sheet 18. I have published the text in my *Chapters of Coming Forth by Day*, pp. 398-402.

of the winds, who dost magnify those divine beings who are like unto thyself. Stablish thou me, then, and strengthen me, O lord of the funeral chest. Grant thou that I may enter into the land of everlastingness, even as it was granted unto thee, and unto thy father Temu, O thou whose body did not see corruption, and who thyself never sawest corruption. I have never wrought that which thou hatest, nay, I have uttered acclamations with those who have loved thy KA. Let not my body turn into worms, but deliver me [from them] even as thou didst deliver thyself. I beseech thee, let me not fall into rottenness as thou dost let every god, and every goddess, and every animal, and every reptile to see corruption when the soul hath gone forth from them after their death. For when the soul departeth, a man seeth corruption, and the bones of his body rot and become wholly loathsomeness, the members decay piecemeal, the bones crumble into an inert mass, the flesh turneth into fœtid liquid, and he becometh a brother unto the decay which cometh upon him. And he turneth into a host of worms, and he becometh a mass of worms, and an end is made of him, and he perisheth in the sight of the god Shu even as doth every god, and every goddess, and every feathered fowl, and every fish, and every creeping thing, and every reptile, and every animal, and every thing whatsoever. When the worms see me and know me, let them fall upon their bellies, and

THE DECEASED IDENTIFIED WITH KHEPERA. 75

let the fear of me terrify them; and thus let it be with every creature after [my] death, whether it be animal, or bird, or fish, or worm, or reptile. And let life arise out of death. Let not decay caused by any reptile make an end [of me], and let not them come against me in their various forms. Do not thou give me over unto that slaughterer who dwelleth in his torture-chamber (?), who killeth the members of the body and maketh them to rot, who worketh destruction upon many dead bodies, whilst he himself remaineth hidden and liveth by slaughter; let me live and perform his message, and let me do that which is commanded by him. Give me not over unto his fingers, and let him not gain the mastery over me, for I am under thy command, O lord of the gods.

"Homage to thee, O my divine father Osiris, thou hast thy being with thy members. Thou didst not decay, thou didst not become worms, thou didst not diminish, thou didst not become corruption, thou didst not putrefy, and thou didst not turn into worms."

The deceased then identifying himself with Khepera, the god who created Osiris and his company of gods, says:—

"I am the god Khepera, and my members shall have an everlasting existence. I shall not decay, I shall not rot, I shall not putrefy, I shall not turn into worms, and I shall not see corruption under the eye of the god Shu. I shall have my being, I shall have my being; I shall live, I shall live; I shall germinate, I shall germinate, I shall germinate; I shall wake up in peace. I shall not putrefy; my bowels shall not perish; I shall not suffer injury; mine eye shall not decay; the form of my countenance shall not disappear; mine ear shall not become deaf; my head shall not be separated from my neck; my tongue shall not be carried away; my hair shall not be cut off; mine eyebrows shall not be shaved off, and no baleful injury shall come upon me. My body shall be stablished, and it shall neither fall into ruin nor be destroyed on this earth."

Judging from such passages as those given above we might think that certain of the Egyptians expected a resurrection of the physical body, and the mention of the various members of the body seems to make this view certain. But the body of which the incorruption and immortality are so strongly declared is the SĀHU, or spiritual body, that sprang into existence out of the physical body, which had become transformed by means of the prayers that had been recited and the ceremonies that had been performed on the day of the funeral, or on that wherein it was laid in the tomb. It is interesting to notice that no mention is made of meat or drink in the CLIVth Chapter, and the only thing which the deceased refers to as necessary for his existence is air, which he obtains through the god Temu, the god who is always depicted in human form; the god is here mentioned in his aspect of the

MUTILATION OF THE BODY AFTER DEATH. 77

night Sun as opposed to Rā the day Sun, and a comparison of the Sun's daily death with the death of the deceased is intended to be made. The deposit of the head of the God-man Osiris at Abydos has already been mentioned, and the belief that it was preserved there was common throughout Egypt. But in the text quoted above the deceased says, "My head shall not be separated from my neck," which seems to indicate that he wished to keep his body whole, notwithstanding that Osiris was almighty, and could restore the limbs and reconstitute the body, even as he had done for his own limbs and body which had been hacked to pieces by Set. Chapter XLIII of the Book of the Dead[1] also has an important reference to the head of Osiris. It is entitled "The Chapter of not letting the head of a man be cut off from him in the underworld," and must be of considerable antiquity. In it the deceased says: "I am the Great One, the son of the Great One; I am Fire, and the son of the Fire, to whom was given his head after it had been cut off. The head of Osiris was not taken away from him, let not the head of the deceased be taken away from him. I have knit myself together (*or* reconstituted myself); I have made myself whole and complete; I have renewed my youth; I am Osiris, the lord of eternity."

From the above it would seem that, according to

[1] See *The Chapters of Coming Forth by Day*, p. 98.

one version of the Osiris story, the head of Osiris was not only cut off, but that it was passed through the fire also; and if this version be very ancient, as it well may be and probably is, it takes us back to prehistoric times in Egypt when the bodies of the dead were mutilated and burned. Prof. Wiedemann thinks [1] that the mutilation and breaking of the bodies of the dead were the results of the belief that in order to make the KA, or "double," leave this earth, the body to which it belonged must be broken, and he instances the fact that objects of every kind were broken at the time when they were placed in the tombs. He traces also a transient custom in the prehistoric graves of Egypt where the methods of burying the body whole and broken into pieces seem to be mingled, for though in some of them the body has been broken into pieces, it is evident that successful attempts have been made to reconstitute it by laying the pieces as far as possible in their proper places. And it may be this custom which is referred to in various places in the Book of the Dead, when the deceased declares that he has collected his limbs "and made his body whole again," and already in the Vth dynasty King Teta is thus addressed—" Rise up, O thou Teta! Thou hast received thy head, thou hast knitted together thy bones,[2] thou hast collected thy members."

[1] See J. de Morgan, *Ethnographie Préhistorique*, p. 210.
[2] *Recueil de Travaux*, tom. v. p. 40 (l. 287).

PERSISTENCE OF OSIRIS WORSHIP.

The history of Osiris, the god of the resurrection, has now been traced from the earliest times to the end of the period of the rule of the priests of Amen (about B.C. 900), by which time Amen-Rā had been thrust in among the gods of the underworld, and prayers were made, in some cases, to him instead of to Osiris. From this time onwards Amen maintained this exalted position, and in the Ptolemaic period, in an address to the deceased Kerāsher we read "Thy face shineth before Rā, thy soul liveth before Amen, and thy body is renewed before Osiris." And again it is said, "Amen is nigh unto thee to make thee to live again. . . .. Amen cometh to thee having the breath of life, and he causeth thee to draw thy breath within thy funeral house." But in spite of this, Osiris kept and held the highest place in the minds of the Egyptians, from first to last, as the God-man, the being who was both divine and human; and no foreign invasion, and no religious or political disturbances, and no influence which any outside peoples could bring to bear upon them, succeeded in making them regard the god as anything less than the cause and symbol and type of the resurrection, and of the life everlasting. For about five thousand years men were mummified in imitation of the mummied form of Osiris; and they went to their graves believing that their bodies would vanquish the powers of death, and the grave, and decay, because Osiris had vanquished them; and they had certain hope of the resurrection in an immortal, eternal, and spiritual body, because Osiris had risen in a transformed spiritual body, and had ascended into heaven, where he had become the king and the judge of the dead, and had attained unto everlasting life therein.

The chief reason for the persistence of the worship of Osiris in Egypt was, probably, the fact that it promised both resurrection and eternal life to its followers. Even after the Egyptians had embraced Christianity they continued to mummify their dead, and for long after they continued to mingle the attributes of their God and the "gods" with those of God Almighty and Christ. The Egyptians of their own will never got away from the belief that the body must be mummified if eternal life was to be assured to the dead, but the Christians, though preaching the same doctrine of the resurrection as the Egyptians, went a step further, and insisted that there was no need to mummify the dead at all. St. Anthony the Great besought his followers not to embalm his body and keep it in a house, but to bury it and to tell no man where it had been buried, lest those who loved him should come and draw it forth, and mummify it as they were wont to do to the bodies of those whom they regarded as saints. "For long past," he said, "I have entreated the bishops and preachers to exhort the people not to continue to observe this useless custom";

DEATH OF OSIRIS WORSHIP.

and concerning his own body, he said, "At the resurrection of the dead I shall receive it from the Saviour incorruptible."[1] The spread of this idea gave the art of mummifying its death-blow, and though from innate conservatism, and the love of having the actual bodies of their beloved dead near them, the Egyptians continued for a time to preserve their dead as before, yet little by little the reasons for mummifying were forgotten, the knowledge of the art died out, the funeral ceremonies were curtailed, the prayers became a dead letter, and the custom of making mummies became obsolete. With the death of the art died also the belief in and the worship of Osiris, who from being the god of the dead became a dead god, and to the Christians of Egypt, at least, his place was filled by Christ, "the firstfruits of them that slept," Whose resurrection and power to grant eternal life were at that time being preached throughout most of the known world. In Osiris the Christian Egyptians found the prototype of Christ, and in the pictures and statues of Isis suckling her son Horus, they perceived the prototypes of the Virgin Mary and her Child. Never did Christianity find elsewhere in the world a people whose minds were so thoroughly well prepared to receive its doctrines as the Egyptians.

This chapter may be fittingly ended by a few

[1] See Rosweyde, *Vitae Patrum*, p. 59; *Life of St. Anthony*, by Athanasius (Migne), *Patrologiæ*, Ser. Graec. tom. 26, col. 972.

extracts from the *Songs of Isis and Nephthys*, which were sung in the Temple of Amen-Rā at Thebes by two priestesses who personified the two goddesses.[1]

"Hail, thou lord of the underworld, thou Bull of those who are therein, thou 'Image of Rā-Harmachis, thou Babe of beautiful appearance, come thou to us in peace. Thou didst repel thy disasters, thou didst drive away evil hap; Lord, come to us in peace. O Un-nefer, lord of food, thou chief, thou who art of terrible majesty, thou God, president of the gods, when thou dost inundate the land [all] things are engendered. Thou art gentler than the gods. The emanations of thy body make the dead and the living to live, O thou lord of food, thou prince of green herbs, thou mighty lord, thou staff of life, thou giver of offerings to the gods, and of sepulchral meals to the blessed dead. Thy soul flieth after Rā, thou shinest at dawn, thou settest at twilight, thou risest every day; thou shalt rise on the left hand of Atmu for ever and ever. Thou art the glorious one, the vicar of Rā; the company of the gods cometh to thee invoking thy face, the flame whereof reacheth unto thine enemies. We rejoice when thou gatherest together thy bones, and when thou hast made whole thy body daily. Anubis cometh to thee, and the two sisters (*i.e.*, Isis and Nephthys) come to thee. They have obtained beautiful things for thee, and they gather

[1] See my *Hieratic Papyrus of Nesi-Amsu* (*Archæologia*, vol. lii.)

together thy limbs for thee, and they seek to put together the mutilated members of thy body. Wipe thou the impurities which are on them upon our hair and come thou to us having no recollection of that which hath caused thee sorrow. Come thou in thy attribute of 'Prince of the earth,' lay aside thy trepidation and be at peace with us, O Lord. Thou shalt be proclaimed heir of the world, and the One god, and the fulfiller of the designs of the gods. All the gods invoke thee, come therefore to thy temple and be not afraid. O Râ (*i.e.*, Osiris), thou art beloved of Isis and Nephthys; rest thou in thy habitation for ever."

CHAPTER III.

THE "GODS" OF THE EGYPTIANS.

THROUGHOUT this book we have had to refer frequently to the "gods" of Egypt; it is now time to explain who and what they were. We have already shown how much the monotheistic side of the Egyptian religion resembles that of modern Christian nations, and it will have come as a surprise to some that a people, possessing such exalted ideas of God as the Egyptians, could ever have become the byword they did through their alleged worship of a multitude of "gods" in various forms. It is quite true that the Egyptians paid honour to a number of gods, a number so large that the list of their mere names would fill a volume, but it is equally true that the educated classes in Egypt at all times never placed the "gods" on the same high level as God, and they never imagined that their views on this point could be mistaken. In prehistoric times every little village or town, every district and province, and every great city, had its own particular god; we may go a step farther, and say that every family of any wealth and position had its own god. The wealthy family selected some one to attend to its god, and to minister unto his wants, and the poor family contributed, according to its means, towards a common fund for providing a dwelling-house for the god, and for vestments, etc. But the god was an integral part of the family, whether rich or poor, and its destiny was practically locked up with that of the family. The overthrow of the family included the overthrow of the god, and seasons of prosperity resulted in abundant offerings, new vestments, perhaps a new shrine, and the like. The god of the village, although he was a more important being, might be led into captivity along with the people of the village, but the victory of his followers in a raid or fight caused the honours paid to him to be magnified and enhanced his renown.

The gods of provinces or of great cities were, of course, greater than those of villages and private families, and in the large houses dedicated to them, *i.e.*, temples, a considerable number of them, represented by statues, would be found. Sometimes the attributes of one god would be ascribed to another, sometimes two or more gods would be "fused" or united and form one, sometimes gods were imported from remote villages and towns and even from foreign countries, and occasionally a community or town would repudiate its god or gods, and adopt a brand new set from some neighbouring district. Thus the number of the gods was always changing, and the relative position of individual gods was always changing; an obscure, and almost unknown, local god to-day might through a victory in war become the chief god of a city, and on the other hand, a god worshipped with abundant offerings and great ceremony one month might sink into insignificance and become to all intents and purposes a dead god the next. But besides family and village gods there were national gods, and gods of rivers and mountains, and gods of earth and sky, all of which taken together made a formidable number of "divine" beings whose good-will had to be secured, and whose ill-will must be appeased. Besides these, a number of animals as being sacred to the gods were also considered to be "divine," and fear as well as love made the Egyptians add to their numerous classes of gods.

The gods of Egypt whose names are known to us do not represent all those that have been conceived by the Egyptian imagination, for with them as with much else, the law of the survival of the fittest holds good. Of the gods of the prehistoric man we know nothing, but it is more than probable that some of the gods who were worshipped in dynastic times represent, in a modified form, the deities of the savage, or semi-savage, Egyptian that held their influence on his mind the longest. A typical example of such a god will suffice, namely Thoth, whose original emblem was the dog-headed ape. In very early times great respect was paid to this animal on account of his sagacity, intelligence, and cunning; and the simple-minded Egyptian, when he heard him chattering just before the sunrise and sunset, assumed that he was in some way holding converse or was intimately connected with the sun. This idea clung to his mind, and we find in dynastic times, in the vignette representing the rising sun, that the apes, who are said to be the transformed openers of the portals of heaven, form a veritable company of the gods, and at the same time one of the most striking features of the scene. Thus an idea which came into being in the most remote times passed on from generation to generation until it became crystallized in the best copies of the Book of the Dead, at a period when Egypt was at its zenith of power and glory. The peculiar species of the dog-headed ape which is represented in statues and on papyri is famous for its cunning, and it was the words which it supplied to Thoth, who in turn transmitted them to Osiris, that enabled Osiris to be "true of voice," or triumphant, over his enemies. It is probably in this capacity, *i.e.*, as the friend of the dead, that the dog-headed ape appears seated upon the top of the standard of the Balance in which the heart of the deceased is being weighed against the feather symbolic of Maāt; for the commonest titles of the god are "lord of divine books," "lord of divine words," *i.e.*, the formulæ which make the deceased to be obeyed by friend and foe alike in the next world. In later times, when Thoth came to be represented by the ibis bird, his attributes were multiplied, and he became the god of letters, science, mathematics, etc.; at the creation he seems to have played a part not unlike that of "wisdom" which is so beautifully described by the writer of Proverbs (see Chap. VIII. vv. 23–31).

Whenever and wherever the Egyptians attempted to set up a system of gods they always found that the old local gods had to be taken into consideration, and a place had to be found for them in the system. This might be done by making them members of triads, or of groups of nine gods, now commonly called "enneads"; but in one form or other they had to appear. The researches made during the last few years have shown that there must have been several large schools of theological thought in Egypt, and of each of these the priests did their utmost to proclaim the superiority of their gods. In dynastic times there must have been great colleges at Heliopolis, Memphis, Abydos, and one or more places in the Delta, not to mention the smaller schools of priests which probably existed at places on both sides of the Nile from Memphis to the south. Of the theories and doctrines of all such schools and colleges, those of Heliopolis have survived in the completest form, and by careful examination of the funeral texts which were inscribed on the monuments of the kings of Egypt of the Vth and VIth dynasties we can say what views they held about many of the gods. At the outset we see that the great god of Heliopolis was Temu or Atmu, the setting sun, and to him the priests of that place ascribed the attributes which rightly belong to Rā, the Sun-god of the day-time. For some reason or other they formulated the idea of a company of the gods, nine in number, which was called the "great company (*paut*) of the gods," and at the head of this company they placed the god Temu. In Chapter XVII of the Book of the Dead[1] we find the following passage:—

"I am the god Temu in his rising; I am the only One. I came into being in Nu. I am Rā who rose in the beginning."

Next comes the question, "But who is this?" And the answer is: "It is Rā when at the beginning he rose in the city of Suten-henen (Heracleopolis Magna) crowned like a king in rising. The pillars of the god Shu were not as yet created when he was upon the staircase of him that dwelleth in Khemennu (Hermopolis Magna)." From these statements we learn that Temu and Rā were one and the same god, and that he was the first offspring of the god Nu, the primeval watery mass, out of which all the gods

[1] See *Chapters of Coming Forth by Day*, p. 49.

came into being. The text continues: "I am the great god Nu who gave birth to himself, and who made his names to come into being and to form the company of the gods. But who is this? It is Rā, the creator of the names of his members which came into being in the form of the gods who are in the train of Rā." And again: "I am he who is not driven back among the gods. But who is this? It is Tem, the dweller in his disk, or as others say, it is Rā in his rising in the eastern horizon of heaven." Thus we learn further that Nu was self-produced, and that the gods are simply the names of his limbs; but then Rā is Nu, and the gods who are in his train or following are merely personifications of the names of his own members. He who cannot be driven back among the gods is either Temu or Rā, and so we find that Nu, Temu, and Rā are one and the same god. The priests of Heliopolis in setting Temu at the head of their company of the gods thus gave Rā, and Nu also, a place of high honour; they cleverly succeeded in making their own local god chief of the company, but at the same time they provided the older gods with positions of importance. In this way worshippers of Rā, who had regarded their god as the oldest of the gods, would have little cause to complain of the introduction of Temu into the company of the gods, and the local vanity of Heliopolis would be gratified.

But besides the nine gods who were supposed to

form the "great company" of gods of the city of Heliopolis, there was a second group of nine gods called the "little company" of the gods, and yet a third group of nine gods, which formed the least company. Now although the *paut* or company of nine gods might be expected to contain nine always, this was not the case, and the number nine thus applied is sometimes misleading. There are several passages extant in texts in which the gods of a *paut* are enumerated, but the total number is sometimes ten and sometimes eleven. This fact is easily explained when we remember that the Egyptians deified the various forms or aspects of a god, or the various phases in his life. Thus the setting sun, called Temu or Atmu, and the rising sun, called Khepera, and the mid-day sun, called Rā, were three forms of the same god; and if any one of these three forms was included in a *paut* or company of nine gods, the other two forms were also included by implication, even though the *paut* then contained eleven instead of nine gods. Similarly, the various forms of each god or goddess of the *paut* were understood to be included in it, however large the total number of gods might become. We are not, therefore, to imagine that the three companies of the gods were limited in number to 9 × 3, or twenty-seven, even though the symbol for god be given twenty-seven times in the texts.

We have already alluded to the great number of

gods who were known to the Egyptians, but it will be readily imagined that it was only those who were thought to deal with man's destiny, here and hereafter, who obtained the worship and reverence of the people of Egypt. These were, comparatively, limited in number, and in fact may be said to consist of the members of the great company of the gods of Heliopolis, that is to say, of the gods who belonged to the cycle of Osiris. These may be briefly described as follows:—

1. TEMU or ATMU, *i.e.*, the "closer" of the day, just as Ptah was the "opener" of the day. In the story of the creation he declares that he evolved himself under the form of the god Khepera, and in hymns he is said to be the "maker of the gods," "the creator of men," etc., and he usurped the position of Rā among the gods of Egypt. His worship must have been already very ancient at the time of the kings of the Vth dynasty, for his traditional form is that of a man at that time.

2. SHU was the firstborn son of Temu. According to one legend he sprang direct from the god, and according to another the goddess Hathor was his mother; yet a third legend makes him the son of Temu by the goddess Iusāset. He it was who made his way between the gods Seb and Nut and raised up the latter to form the sky, and this belief is commemorated by the figures of this god in which he is represented as a god raising himself up from the earth with the sun's disk on his shoulders. As a

power of nature he typified the light, and, standing on the top of a staircase at Hermopolis Magna,[1] he raised up the sky and held it up during each day. To assist him in this work he placed a pillar at each of the cardinal points, and the "supports of Shu" are thus the props of the sky.

3. TEFNUT was the twin-sister of Shu; as a power of nature she typified moisture or some aspect of the sun's heat, but as a god of the dead she seems to have been, in some way, connected with the supply of drink to the deceased. Her brother Shu was the right eye of Temu, and she was the left, *i.e.*, Shu represented an aspect of the Sun, and Tefnut of the Moon. The gods Temu, Shu, and Tefnut thus formed a trinity, and in the story of the creation the god Temu says, after describing how Shu and Tefnut proceeded from himself, "thus from being one god I became three."

4. SEB was the son of the god Shu. He is called the "Erpā," *i.e.*, the "hereditary chief" of the gods, and the "father of the gods," these being, of course, Osiris, Isis, Set, and Nephthys. He was originally the god of the earth, but later he became a god of the dead as representing the earth wherein the deceased was laid. One legend identifies him with the goose, the bird which in later times was sacred to him, and he is often called the "Great Cackler," in allusion

---

[1] See above, pp. 69 and 89.

to the idea that he made the primeval egg from which the world came into being.

5. NUT was the wife of Seb and the mother of Osiris, Isis, Set, and Nephthys. Originally she was the personification of the sky, and represented the feminine principle which was active at the creation of the universe. According to an old view, Seb and Nut existed in the primeval watery abyss side by side with Shu and Tefnut; and later Seb became the earth and Nut the sky. These deities were supposed to unite every evening, and to remain embraced until the morning, when the god Shu separated them, and set the goddess of the sky upon his four pillars until the evening. Nut was, naturally, regarded as the mother of the gods and of all things living, and she and her husband Seb were considered to be the givers of food, not only to the living but also to the dead. Though different views were current in Egypt as to the exact location of the heaven of the beatified dead, yet all schools of thought in all periods assigned it to some region in the sky, and the abundant allusions in the texts to the heavenly bodies—that is, the sun, moon, and stars—which the deceased dwells with, prove that the final abode of the souls of the righteous was not upon earth. The goddess Nut is sometimes represented as a female along whose body the sun travels, and sometimes as a cow; the tree sacred to her was the sycamore.

OSIRIS AND ISIS.

6. OSIRIS was the son of Seb and Nut, the husband of Isis and the father of Horus. The history of this god is given elsewhere in this book so fully that it is only necessary to refer briefly to him. He was held to be a man although of divine origin; he lived and reigned as a king on this earth; he was treacherously murdered by his brother Set, and his body was cut up into fourteen pieces, which were scattered about Egypt; after his death, Isis, by the use of magical formulæ supplied to her by Thoth, succeeded in raising him to life, and he begot a son called Horus; when Horus was grown up, he engaged in combat with Set, and overcame him, and thus "avenged his father"; by means of magical formulæ, supplied to him by Thoth, Osiris reconstituted and revivified his body, and became the type of the resurrection and the symbol of immortality; he was also the hope, the judge, and the god of the dead, probably even in pre-dynastic times. Osiris was in one aspect a solar deity, and originally he seems to have represented the sun after it had set; but he is also identified with the moon. In the XVIIIth dynasty, however, he is already the equal of Rā, and later the attributes of God and of all the "gods" were ascribed to him.

7. ISIS was the wife of Osiris and mother of Horus; as a nature goddess she had a place in the boat of the sun at the creation, when she probably typified the dawn. By reason of her success in revivifying her

husband's body by means of the utterance of magical formulæ, she is called the "lady of enchantments." Her wanderings in search of her husband's body, and the sorrow which she endured in bringing forth and rearing her child in the papyrus swamps of the Delta, and the persecution which she suffered at the hands of her husband's enemies, form the subject of many allusions in texts of all periods. She has various aspects, but the one which appealed most to the imagination of the Egyptians, was that of "divine mother"; in this character thousands of statues represent her seated and suckling her child Horus whom she holds upon her knees.

8. SET was the son of Seb and Nut, and the husband of Nephthys. At a very early period he was regarded as the brother and friend of "Horus the Elder," the Aroueris of the Greeks, and Set represented the night whilst Horus represented the day. Each of these gods performed many offices of a friendly nature for the dead, and among others they set up and held the ladder by which the deceased made his way from this earth to heaven, and helped him to ascend it. But, at a later period, the views of the Egyptians concerning Set changed, and soon after the reign of the kings called "Seti," *i.e.*, those whose names were based upon that of the god, he became the personification of all evil, and of all that is horrible and terrible in nature, such as the desert in its most desolate form, the storm and the

tempest, etc. Set, as a power of nature, was always waging war with Horus the Elder, *i.e.*, the night did battle with the day for supremacy; both gods, however, sprang from the same source, for the heads of both are, in one scene, made to belong to one body. When Horus, the son of Isis, had grown up, he did battle with Set, who had murdered Horus's father Osiris, and vanquished him; in many texts these two originally distinct fights are confused, and the two Horus gods also. The conquest of Set by Horus in the first conflict typified only the defeat of the night by the day, but the defeat of Set in the second seems to have been understood as the victory of life over death, and of good over evil. The symbol of Set was an animal with a head something like that of a camel, but it has not yet been satisfactorily identified; figures of the god are uncommon, for most of them were destroyed by the Egyptians when they changed their views about him.

9. NEPHTHYS was the sister of Isis and her companion in all her wanderings and troubles; like her she had a place in the boat of the Sun at creation, when she probably typified the twilight or very early night. She was, according to one legend, the mother of Anubis by Osiris, but in the texts his father is declared to be Rā. In funeral papyri, stelæ, etc., she always accompanies Isis in her ministrations to the dead, and as she assisted Osiris and Isis to defeat the wickedness

of her own husband (Set), so she helped the deceased to overcome the powers of death and the grave.

Here then we have the nine gods of the divine company of Heliopolis, but no mention is made of Horus, the son of Isis, who played such an important part in the history of his father Osiris, and nothing is said about Thoth; both gods are, however, included in the company in various passages of the text, and it may be that their omission from it is the result of an error of the scribe. We have already given the chief details of the history of the gods Horus and Thoth, and the principal gods of the other companies may now be briefly named.

Nu was the "father of the gods," and progenitor of the "great company of the gods"; he was the primeval watery mass out of which all things came.

PTAH was one of the most active of the three great gods who carried out the commands of Thoth, who gave expression in words to the will of the primeval, creative Power; he was self-created, and was a form of the Sun-god Rā as the "Opener" of the day. From certain allusions in the Book of the Dead he is known to have "opened the mouth"[1] of the gods, and it is in this capacity that he became a god of the cycle of Osiris. His feminine counterpart was the goddess

[1] "May the god Ptah open my mouth"; "may the god Shu open my mouth with his implement of iron wherewith he opened the mouth of the gods" (Chap. XXIII.)

SEKHET, and the third member of the triad of which he was the chief was NEFER-TEMU.

PTAH-SEKER is the dual god formed by fusing Seker, the Egyptian name of the incarnation of the Apis Bull of Memphis, with Ptah.

PTAH-SEKER-AUSAR was a triune god who, in brief, symbolized life, death, and the resurrection.

KHNEMU was one of the old cosmic gods who assisted Ptah in carrying out the commands of Thoth, who gave expression in words to the will of the primeval, creative Power, he is described as "the maker of things which are, the creator of things which shall be, the source of created things, the father of fathers, and the mother of mothers." It was he who, according to one legend, fashioned man upon a potter's wheel.

KHEPERA was an old primeval god, and the type of matter which contains within itself the germ of life which is about to spring into a new existence; thus he represented the dead body from which the spiritual body was about to rise. He is depicted in the form of a man having a beetle for a head, and this insect became his emblem because it was supposed to be self-begotten and self-produced. To the present day certain of the inhabitants of the Sûdân pound the dried scarabæus or beetle and drink it in water, believing that it will insure them a numerous progeny. The name "Khepera" means "he who rolls," and when the insect's habit of rolling along its ball filled with eggs is taken into consideration, the appropriateness of the name is apparent. As the ball of eggs rolls along the germs mature and burst into life; and as the sun rolls across the sky emitting light and heat and with them life, so earthly things are produced and have their being by virtue thereof.

RĀ was probably the oldest of the gods worshipped in Egypt, and his name belongs to such a remote period that its meaning is unknown. He was in all periods the visible emblem of God, and was the god of this earth to whom offerings and sacrifices were made daily; time began when Rā appeared above the horizon at creation in the form of the Sun, and the life of a man was compared to his daily course at a very early date. Rā was supposed to sail over heaven in two boats, the ĀTET or MĀTET boat in which he journeyed from sunrise until noon, and the SEKTET boat in which he journeyed from noon until sunset. At his rising he was attacked by Āpep, a mighty "dragon" or serpent, the type of evil and darkness, and with this monster he did battle until the fiery darts which he discharged into the body of Āpep scorched and burnt him up; the fiends that were in attendance upon this terrible foe were also destroyed by fire, and their bodies were hacked in pieces. A repetition of this story is given in the legend of the fight between Horus and Set, and in both forms it represented originally the fight which was supposed to go on daily between light and darkness. Later, however, when Osiris had usurped the position of Rā, and Horus represented a divine power who was about to avenge the cruel murder of his father, and the wrong which had been done to him, the moral conceptions of right and wrong, good and evil, truth and falsehood were applied to light and darkness, that is to say, to Horus and Set.

As Rā was the "father of the gods," it was natural that every god should represent some phase of him, and that he should represent every god. A good illustration of this fact is afforded by a Hymn to Rā, a fine copy of which is found inscribed on the walls of the sloping corridor in the tomb of Seti I., about B.C. 1370, from which we quote the following:—

11. "Praise be unto thee, O Rā, thou exalted Power, who dost enter into the habitations of Ament, behold [thy] body is Temu.

12. "Praise be unto thee, O Rā, thou exalted Power, who dost enter into the hidden place of Anubis, behold [thy] body is Khepera.

13. "Praise be unto thee, O Rā, thou exalted Power, whose duration of life is greater than that of the hidden forms, behold [thy] body is Shu.

14. "Praise be unto thee, O Rā, thou exalted Power, . . . behold [thy] body is Tefnut.

15. "Praise be unto thee, O Rā, thou exalted Power, who bringest forth green things in their season, behold [thy] body is Seb.

16. "Praise be unto thee, O Rā, thou exalted Power, thou mighty being who dost judge,... behold [thy] body is Nut.

17. "Praise be unto thee, O Rā, thou exalted Power, the lord ... behold [thy] body is Isis.

18. "Praise be unto thee, O Rā, thou exalted Power, whose head giveth light to that which is in front of thee, behold [thy] body is Nephthys.

19. "Praise be unto thee, O Rā, thou exalted Power, thou source of the divine members, thou One, who bringest into being that which hath been begotten, behold [thy] body is Horus.

20. "Praise be unto thee, O Rā, thou exalted Power, who dost dwell in and illumine the celestial deep, behold [thy] body is Nu."[1]

In the paragraphs which follow Rā is identified with a large number of gods and divine personages whose names are not of such common occurrence in the texts as those given above, and in one way or another the attributes of all the gods are ascribed to him. At the time when the hymn was written it is clear that polytheism, not pantheism as some would have it, was in the ascendant, and notwithstanding the fact

[1] For the text see *Annales du Musée Guimet: Le Tombeau de Sėti I.* (ed. Lefébure), Paris, 1886, pl. v.

RISE OF AMEN WORSHIP.

that the Theban god Amen was gradually being forced to the headship of the companies of the gods of Egypt, we find everywhere the attempt being made to emphasize the view that every god, whether foreign or native, was an aspect or form of Rā.

The god Amen just referred to was originally a local god of Thebes, whose shrine was either founded or rebuilt as far back as the XIIth dynasty, about B.C. 2500. This "hidden" god, for such is the meaning of the name Amen, was essentially a god of the south of Egypt, but when the Theban kings vanquished their foes in the north, and so became masters of the whole country, Amen became a god of the first importance, and the kings of the XVIIIth, XIXth, and XXth dynasties endowed his temples on a lavish scale. The priests of the god called Amen "the king of the gods," and they endeavoured to make all Egypt accept him as such, but in spite of their power they saw that they could not bring this result about unless they identified him with the oldest gods of the land. They declared that he represented the hidden and mysterious power which created and sustains the universe, and that the sun was the symbol of this power; they therefore added his name to that of Rā, and in this form he gradually usurped the attributes and powers of Nu, Khnemu, Ptah, Hāpi, and other great gods. A revolt headed by Amen-hetep, or Amenophis IV. (about B.C. 1500), took place against the supremacy of Amen in the middle of the XVIIIth dynasty, but it was unsuccessful. This king hated the god and his name so strongly that he changed his own name into that of "Khu-en-Aten," *i.e.*, "the glory of the solar Disk," and ordered the name of Amen to be obliterated, wherever possible, on temples and other great monuments; and this was actually done in many places. It is impossible to say exactly what the religious views of the king were, but it is certain that he wished to substitute the cult of Aten, a form of the Sun-god worshipped at Annu (*i.e.*, On or Heliopolis) in very ancient times, for that of Amen. "Aten" means literally the "Disk of the Sun," and though it is difficult to understand at this distance of time in what the difference between the worship of Rā and the worship of "Rā in his Disk" consisted, we may be certain that there must have been some subtle, theological distinction between them. But whatever the difference may have been, it was sufficient to make Amenophis forsake the old capital Thebes and withdraw to a place [1] some distance to the north of that city, where he carried on the worship of his beloved god Aten. In the pictures of the Aten worship which have come down to us the god appears in the form of a disk from which proceed a number of arms and hands that bestow life upon his worshippers. After the death of Amenophis the cult of Aten

[1] The site is marked by the ruins of Tell el-Amarna.

declined, and Amen resumed his sway over the minds of the Egyptians.

Want of space forbids the insertion here of a full list of the titles of Amen, and a brief extract from the Papyrus of the Princess Nesi-Khensu [1] must suffice to describe the estimation in which the god was held about B.C. 1000. In this Amen is addressed as "the holy god, the lord of all the gods, Amen-Rā, the lord of the thrones of the world, the prince of Apt (*i.e.*, Karnak), the holy soul who came into being in the beginning, the great god who liveth by right and truth, the first ennead who gave birth unto the other two enneads,[2] the being in whom every god existeth, the One of One, the creator of the things which came into being when the earth took form in the beginning, whose births are hidden, whose forms are manifold, and whose growth cannot be known. The holy Form, beloved and terrible and mighty . . . the lord of space, the mighty One of the form of Khepera, who came into existence through Khepera, the lord of the form of Khepera; when he came into being nothing existed except himself. He shone upon the earth from primeval time, he the Disk, the prince of light and radiance. . . . When this holy god moulded himself, the heavens and the earth were made by his heart (*or* mind). . . . He

---

[1] For a hieroglyphic transcript of the hieratic text, see Maspero, *Mémoires*, tom. i., p. 594 ff.

[2] *I.e.*, the great, the little, and the least companies of the gods; each company (*paut*) contained nine gods.

is the Disk of the Moon, the beauties whereof pervade the heavens and the earth, the untiring and beneficent king whose will germinateth from rising to setting, from whose divine eyes men and women come forth, and from whose mouth the gods do come, and [by whom] food and meat and drink are made and provided, and [by whom] the things which exist are created. He is the lord of time, and he traverseth eternity; he is the aged one who reneweth his youth. . . . He is the Being who cannot be known, and he is more hidden than all the gods. . . . He giveth long life and multiplieth the years of those who are favoured by him, he is the gracious protector of him whom he setteth in his heart, and he is the fashioner of eternity and everlastingness. He is the king of the North and of the South, Amen-Rā, king of the gods, the lord of heaven, and of earth, and of the waters and of the mountains, with whose coming into being the earth began its existence, the mighty one, more princely than all the gods of the first company."

In the above extract, it will be noticed that Amen is called the "One of One," or the "One One," a title which has been explained as having no reference whatever to the unity of God as understood in modern times: but unless these words are intended to express the idea of unity, what is their meaning? It is also said that he is "without second," and thus there is no doubt whatever that when the Egyptians declared their god to be One, and without a second, they meant precisely what the Hebrews and Arabs meant when they declared their God to be One.[1] Such a God was an entirely different Being from the personifications of the powers of nature and the existences which, for want of a better name, have been called "gods."

But, besides Rā, there existed in very early times a god called HORUS, whose symbol was the hawk, which, it seems, was the first living thing worshipped by the Egyptians; Horus was the Sun-god, like Rā, and in later times was confounded with Horus the son of Isis. The chief forms of Horus given in the texts are: (1) HERU-UR (Aroueris), (2) HERU-MERTI, (3) HERU-NUB, (4) HERU-KHENT-KHAT, (5) HERU-KHENT-AN-MAA, (6) HERU-KHUTI, (7) HERU-SAM-TAUI, (8) HERU-HEKENNU, (9) HERU-BEHUTET. Connected with one of the forms of Horus, originally, were the four gods of the cardinal points, or the "four spirits of Horus," who supported heaven at its four corners; their names were HĀPI, TUAMUTEF, AMSET, and QEBHSENNUF, and they represented the north, east, south, and west respectively. The intestines of the dead were embalmed and placed in four jars, each being under the protection of one of these four gods. Other important gods of the dead are: (1) ANUBIS, the son of Rā or Osiris, who presided over the abode of the dead, and with AP-UAT

[1] See Deut., vi. 4; aud *Koran*, chapter cxii.

shared the dominion of the "funeral mountain"; the symbol of each of these gods is a jackal. (2) HU and SA, the children of Temu or Rā, who appear in the boat of the sun at the creation, and later in the Judgment Scene. (3) The goddess MAĀT, who was associated with Thoth, Ptah, and Khnemu in the work of creation; the name means "straight," hence what is right, true, truth, real, genuine, upright, righteous, just, steadfast, unalterable, and the like. (4) The goddess HET-HERT (Hathor), *i.e.*, the "house of Horus," which was that part of the sky where the sun rose and set. The sycamore tree was sacred to her, and the deceased prays to be fed by her with celestial food from out of it (5) The goddess MEH-URT, who represented that portion of the sky in which the sun takes his daily course; here it was, according to the view held at one period at least, that the judgment of the deceased was supposed to take place. (6) NEITH, the mother of SEBEK, who was also a goddess of the eastern portion of the sky. (7) SEKHET and BAST, who are represented with the heads of a lion and a cat, and who were symbols of the destroying, scorching power of the sun, and of the gentle heat thereof, respectively. (8) SERQ, who was a form of Isis. (9) TA-URT (Thoueris), who was the genetrix of the gods. (10) UATCHET, who was a form of Hathor, and who had dominion over the northern sky, just as NEKHEBET was mistress of the southern sky. (11) NEHEB-KA, who was a goddess who possessed

SEBAK, HĀPI, AND AMSU.   109

magical powers, and in some respects resembled Isis in her attributes. (12) SEBAK, who was a form of the Sun-god, and was in later times confounded with Sebak, or Sebek, the friend of Set. (13) AMSU (or MIN or KHEM), who was the personification of the generative and reproductive powers of nature. (14) BEB or BABA, who was the " firstborn son of Osiris." (15) HĀPI, who was the god of the Nile, and with whom most of the great gods were identified.

The names of the beings who at one time or another were called "gods" in Egypt are so numerous that a mere list of them would fill scores of pages, and in a work of this kind would be out of place. The reader is, therefore, referred to Lanzone's *Mitologia Egizia*, where a considerable number are enumerated and described.

CHAPTER IV.

THE JUDGMENT OF THE DEAD.

THE belief that the deeds done in the body would be subjected to an analysis and scrutiny by the divine powers after the death of a man belongs to the earliest period of Egyptian civilization, and this belief remained substantially the same in all generations. Though we have no information as to the locality where the Last Judgment took place, or whether the Egyptian soul passed into the judgment-hall immediately after the death of the body, or after the mummification was ended and the body was deposited in the tomb, it is quite certain that the belief in the judgment was as deeply rooted in the Egyptians as the belief in immortality. There seems to have been no idea of a general judgment when all those who had lived in the world should receive their reward for the deeds done in the body; on the contrary, all the evidence available goes to show that each soul was dealt with individually, and was either permitted to pass into the kingdom of Osiris and of the blessed, or was destroyed straightway. Certain passages in the texts seem to suggest the idea of the existence of a place for departed spirits wherein the souls condemned in the judgment might dwell, but it must be remembered that it was the enemies of Rā, the Sun-god, that inhabited this region; and it is impossible to imagine that the divine powers who presided over the judgment would permit the souls of the wicked to live after they had been condemned and to become enemies of those who were pure and blessed. On the other hand, if we attach any importance to the ideas of the Copts upon this subject, and consider that they represent ancient beliefs which they derived from the Egyptians traditionally, it must be admitted that the Egyptian underworld contained some region wherein the souls of the wicked were punished for an indefinite period. The Coptic lives of saints and martyrs are full of allusions to the sufferings of the damned, but whether the descriptions of these are due to imaginings of the mind of the Christian Egyptian or to the bias of the scribe's opinions cannot always be said. When we consider that the Coptic hell was little more than a modified form of the ancient Egyptian Amenti, or Amentet, it is difficult to believe that it was the name of the Egyptian underworld only which was borrowed, and that the ideas and beliefs concerning it which were held by the ancient Egyptians were not at the same time absorbed. Some Christian writers are most minute in their classification of the wicked in hell, as we may see from the following extract from the life of Pisentios,[1] Bishop of Keft, in the VIIth century of our era. The holy man had taken refuge in a tomb wherein a number of mummies had been piled up, and when he had read the list of the names of the people who had been buried there he gave it to his disciple to replace. Then he addressed his disciple and admonished him to do the work of God with diligence, and warned him that every man must become even as were the mummies which lay before them. "And some," said he, "whose sins have been many are now in Amenti, others are in the outer darkness, others are in pits and ditches filled with fire, and others are in the river of fire: upon these last no one hath bestowed rest. And others, likewise, are in a place of rest, by reason of their good works." When the disciple had departed, the holy man began to talk to one of the mummies who had been a native of the town of Erment, or Armant, and whose father and mother had been called Agricolaos and Eustathia. He had been a worshipper of Poseidon, and had never heard that Christ had come into the world. "And," said he, "woe, woe is me because I was born into the world. Why did not my mother's womb become my tomb? When it became necessary for me to die, the Kosmokratôr angels were the first to come round about me, and they told me of all the sins which

[1] Ed. Amélineau, Paris, 1887, p. 144 f.

I had committed, and they said unto me, 'Let him that can save thee from the torments into which thou shalt be cast come hither.' And they had in their hands iron knives, and pointed goads which were like unto sharp spears, and they drove them into my sides and gnashed upon me with their teeth. When a little time afterwards my eyes were opened I saw death hovering about in the air in its manifold forms, and at that moment angels who were without pity came and dragged my wretched soul from my body, and having tied it under the form of a black horse they led me away to Amenti. Woe be unto every sinner like unto myself who hath been born into the world! O my master and father, I was then delivered into the hands of a multitude of tormentors who were without pity and who had each a different form. Oh, what a number of wild beasts did I see in the way! Oh, what a number of powers were there that inflicted punishment upon me! And it came to pass that when I had been cast into the outer darkness, I saw a great ditch which was more than two hundred cubits deep, and it was filled with reptiles; each reptile had seven heads, and the body of each was like unto that of a scorpion. In this place also lived the Great Worm, the mere sight of which terrified him that looked thereat. In his mouth he had teeth like unto iron stakes, and one took me and threw me to this Worm which never ceased to eat; then immediately all the [other] beasts gathered together near him, and when he had filled his mouth [with my flesh], all the beasts who were round about me filled theirs." In answer to the question of the holy man as to whether he had enjoyed any rest or period without suffering, the mummy replied: "Yea, O my father, pity is shown unto those who are in torment every Saturday and every Sunday. As soon as Sunday is over we are cast into the torments which we deserve, so that we may forget the years which we have passed in the world; and as soon as we have forgotten the grief of this torment we are cast into another which is still more grievous."

Now, it is easy to see from the above description of the torments which the wicked were supposed to suffer, that the writer had in his mind some of the pictures with which we are now familiar, thanks to the excavation of tombs which has gone on in Egypt during the last few years; and it is also easy to see that he, in common with many other Coptic writers, misunderstood the purport of them. The outer darkness, *i.e.*, the blackest place of all in the underworld, the river of fire, the pits of fire, the snake and the scorpion, and such like things, all have their counterparts, or rather originals, in the scenes which accompany the texts which describe the passage of the sun through the underworld during the hours of the night. Having once misunderstood the general meaning of such scenes,

THE SAGE HERUTĀTĀF.

it was easy to convert the foes of Rā, the Sun-god, into the souls of the damned, and to look upon the burning up of such foes—who were after all only certain powers of nature personified — as the well-merited punishment of those who had done evil upon the earth. How far the Copts reproduced unconsciously the views which had been held by their ancestors for thousands of years cannot be said, but even after much allowance has been made for this possibility, there remains still to be explained a large number of beliefs and views which seem to have been the peculiar product of the Egyptian Christian imagination.

It has been said above that the idea of the judgment of the dead is of very great antiquity in Egypt; indeed, it is so old that it is useless to try to ascertain the date of the period when it first grew up. In the earliest religious texts known to us, there are indications that the Egyptians expected a judgment, but they are not sufficiently definite to argue from ; it is certainly doubtful if the judgment was thought to be as thorough and as searching then as in the later period. As far back as the reign of Men-kau-Rā, the Mycerinus of the Greeks, about B.C. 3600, a religious text, which afterwards formed chapter 30B of the Book of the Dead, was found inscribed on an iron slab, in the handwriting of the god Thoth, by the royal son or prince Herutātāf.[1] The original purpose of the composition

[1] See *Chapters of Coming Forth by Day*, Translation, p. 80.

of this text cannot be said, but there is little doubt that it was intended to benefit the deceased in the judgment, and, if we translate its title literally, it was intended to prevent his heart from "falling away from him in the underworld." In the first part of it the deceased, after adjuring his heart, says, "May naught stand up to oppose me in the judgment; may there be no opposition to me in the presence of the sovereign princes; may there be no parting of thee from me in the presence of him that keepeth the Balance! ... May the officers of the court of Osiris (in Egyptian *Shenit*), who form the conditions of the lives of men, not cause my name to stink! Let [the judgment] be satisfactory unto me, let the hearing be satisfactory unto me, and let me have joy of heart at the weighing of words. Let not that which is false be uttered against me before the Great God, the Lord of Amentet."

Now, although the papyrus upon which this statement and prayer are found was written about two thousand years after Men-kau-Rā reigned, there is no doubt that they were copied from texts which were themselves copied at a much earlier period, and that the story of the finding of the text inscribed upon an iron slab is contemporary with its actual discovery by Herutātāf. · It is not necessary to inquire here whether the word "find" (in Egyptian *qem*) means a genuine discovery or not, but it is clear that those who had the papyrus copied saw no absurdity or impropriety in ascribing the text to the period of Men-kau-Rā. Another text, which afterwards also became a chapter of the Book of the Dead, under the title "Chapter of not letting the heart of the deceased be driven away from him in the underworld," was inscribed on a coffin of the XIth dynasty, about B.C. 2500, and in it we have the following petition: "May naught stand up to oppose me in judgment in the presence of the lords of the trial (literally, 'lords of things'); let it not be said of me and of that which I have done, 'He hath done deeds against that which is very right and true'; may naught be against me in the presence of the Great God, the Lord of Amentet."[1] From these passages we are right in assuming that before the end of the IVth dynasty the idea of being "weighed in the balance" was already evolved; that the religious schools of Egypt had assigned to a god the duty of watching the balance when cases were being tried; that this-weighing in the balance took place in the presence of the beings called *Shenit*, who were believed to control the acts and deeds of men; that it was thought that evidence unfavourable to the deceased might be produced by his foes at the judgment; that the weighing took place in the presence of the Great God, the Lord of Amentet; and that the heart of the deceased might fail him either physically or morally. The deceased addresses his heart, calling it his "mother,"

[1] *Chapters of Coming Forth by Day*, p 78.

and next identifies it with his *ka* or double, coupling the mention of the *ka* with the name of the god Khnemu: these facts are exceedingly important, for they prove that the deceased considered his heart to be the source of his life and being, and the mention of the god Khnemu takes the date of the composition back to a period coæval with the beginnings of religious thought in Egypt. It was the god Khnemu who assisted Thoth in performing the commands of God at the creation, and one very interesting sculpture at Philæ shows Khnemu in the act of fashioning man upon a potter's wheel. The deceased, in mentioning Khnemu's name, seems to invoke his aid in the judgment as fashioner of man and as the being who is in some respects responsible for the manner of his life upon earth.

In Chapter 30A there is no mention made of the "guardian of the balance," and the deceased says, "May naught stand up to oppose me in judgment in the presence of the lords of things!" The "lords of things" may be either the "lords of creation," *i.e.*, the great cosmic gods, or the "lords of the affairs [of the hall of judgment]," *i.e.*, of the trial. In this chapter the deceased addresses not Khnemu, but "the gods who dwell in the divine clouds, and who are exalted by reason of their sceptres," that is to say, the four gods of the cardinal points, called Mestha, Hāpi Tuamutef, and Qebhsennuf, who also presided over the chief internal organs of the human body. Here, again, it seems as if the deceased was anxious to make these gods in some way responsible for the deeds done by him in his life, inasmuch as they presided over the organs that were the prime movers of his actions. In any case, he considers them in the light of intercessors, for he beseeches them to "speak fair words unto Rā" on his behalf, and to make him to prosper before the goddess Nehebka. In this case, the favour of Rā, the Sun-god, the visible emblem of the almighty and eternal God, is sought for, and also that of the serpent goddess, whose attributes are not yet accurately defined, but who has much to do with the destinies of the dead. No mention whatever is made of the Lord of Amentet—Osiris.

Before we pass to the consideration of the manner in which the judgment is depicted upon the finest examples of the illustrated papyri, reference must be made to an interesting vignette in the papyri of Nebseni [1] and Amen-neb.[2] In both of these papyri we see a figure of the deceased himself being weighed in the balance against his own heart in the presence of the god Osiris. It seems probable that a belief was current at one time in ancient Egypt concerning the possibility of the body being weighed against the heart, with the view of finding out if the former had obeyed the dictates of the latter; be that as it may, however,

[1] British Museum, No. 9900.   [2] British Museum, No. 9964.

it is quite certain that this remarkable variant of the vignette of Chapter 30B had some special meaning, and, as it occurs in two papyri which date from the XVIIIth dynasty, we are justified in assuming that it represents a belief belonging to a much older period. The judgment here depicted must, in any case, be different from that which forms such a striking scene in the later illustrated papyri of the XVIIIth and following dynasties.

We have now proved that the idea of the judgment of the dead was accepted in religious writings as early as the IVth dynasty, about B.C. 3600, but we have to wait nearly two thousand years before we find it in picture form. Certain scenes which are found in the Book of the Dead as vignettes accompanying certain texts or chapters, *e.g.*, the Fields of Hetep, or the Elysian Fields, are exceedingly old, and are found on sarcophagi of the XIth and XIIth dynasties; but the earliest picture known of the Judgment Scene is not older than the XVIIIth dynasty. In the oldest Theban papyri of the Book of the Dead no Judgment Scene is forthcoming, and when we find it wanting in such authoritative documents as the Papyrus of Nebseni and that of Nu,[1] we must take it for granted that there was some reason for its omission. In the great illustrated papyri in which the Judgment Scene is given in full, it will be noticed that it comes at the

[1] British Museum, No. 10,477.

HYMN SAID TO RĀ AT THE JUDGMENT.

beginning of the work, and that it is preceded by hymns and by a vignette. Thus, in the Papyrus of Ani,[1] we have a hymn to Rā, followed by a vignette representing the sunrise, and a hymn to Osiris; and in the Papyrus of Hunefer,[2] though the hymns are different, the arrangement is the same. We are justified, then, in assuming that the hymns and the Judgment Scene together formed an introductory section to the Book of the Dead, and it is possible that it indicates the existence of the belief, at least during the period of the greatest power of the priests of Amen, from B.C. 1700 to B.C. 800, that the judgment of the dead for the deeds done in the body preceded the admission of the dead into the kingdom of Osiris. As the hymns which accompany the Judgment Scene are fine examples of a high class of devotional compositions, a few translations from some of them are here given.

HYMN TO RĀ.[3]

"Homage to thee, O thou who risest in Nu,[4] and who at thy manifestation dost make the world bright with light; the whole company of the gods sing hymns of praise unto thee after thou hast come forth.

---

[1] British Museum, No. 10,470.
[2] British Museum, No. 9901.
[3] See *The Chapters of Coming Forth by Day*, p 7.
[4] The sky personified.

HYMN SAID TO RĀ AT THE JUDGMENT.

The divine Merti[1] goddesses who minister unto thee cherish thee as King of the North and South, thou beautiful and beloved Man-child. When thou risest men and women live. The nations rejoice in thee, and the Souls of Annu[2] (Heliopolis) sing unto thee songs of joy. The Souls of the city of Pe,[3] and the Souls of the city of Nekhen[4] exalt thee, the apes of dawn adore thee, and all beasts and cattle praise thee with one accord. The goddess Seba overthroweth thine enemies, therefore hast thou rejoicing in thy boat; thy mariners are content thereat. Thou hast attained unto the Ātet boat,[5] and thy heart swelleth with joy. O lord of the gods, when thou didst create them they shouted for joy. The azure goddess Nut doth compass thee on every side, and the god Nu floodeth thee with his rays of light. O cast thou thy light upon me and let me see thy beauties, and when thou goest forth over the earth I will sing praises unto thy fair face. Thou risest in heaven's horizon, and thy disk is adored when it resteth upon the mountain to give life unto the world."

"Thou risest, thou risest, and thou comest forth from the god Nu. Thou dost renew thy youth, and

[1] Literally, the Two Eyes, *i.e.*, Isis and Nephthys.
[2] *I e.*, Rā, Shu, and Tefnut.
[3] Part of the city of Buto (Per-Uatchit). The souls of Pe were Horus, Mestha, Hāpi.
[4] *I.e.*, Horus, Tuamutef, and Qebhsennuf.
[5] *I.e.*, the boat in which the sun travels until noon.

thou dost set thyself in the place where thou wast yesterday. O thou divine Child, who didst create thyself, I am not able [to describe] thee. Thou hast come with thy risings, and thou hast made heaven and earth resplendent with thy rays of pure emerald light. The land of Punt [1] is stablished [to give] the perfumes which thou smellest with thy nostrils. Thou risest, O marvellous Being, in heaven, and the two serpent-goddesses, Merti, are stablished upon thy brow. Thou art the giver of laws, O thou lord of the world and of all the inhabitants thereof; all the gods adore thee."

HYMN TO OSIRIS.[2]

"Glory be to thee, O Osiris Un-nefer, the great god within Abydos, king of eternity and lord of everlastingness, the god who passest through millions of years in thy existence. Thou art the eldest son of the womb of Nut, thou wast engendered by Seb, the Ancestor of the gods, thou art the lord of the Crowns of the North and of the South, and of the lofty white crown. As Prince of the gods and of men thou hast received the crook, and the whip, and the dignity of thy divine fathers. Let thy heart which is in the mountain of Ament [3] be content, for thy son Horus is stablished upon thy throne. Thou art crowned the lord of Tattu (Mendes) and ruler

---

[1] *I.e.*, the land on each side of the Red Sea and North-east Africa.
[2] See *The Chapters of Coming Forth by Day*, p. 11.
[3] *I.e.*, the underworld.

in Abtu (Abydos). Through thee the world waxeth green in triumph before the might of Neb-er-tch'er.[1] Thou leadest in thy train that which is, and that which is not yet, in thy name of 'Ta-her-sta-nef;' thou towest along the earth in thy name of 'Seker;' thou art exceedingly mighty and most terrible in thy name of 'Osiris;' thou endurest for ever and for ever in thy name of 'Un-nefer.'"

"Homage to thee, O thou King of kings, Lord of lords, Prince of Princes! From the womb of Nut thou hast ruled the world and the underworld. Thy body is of bright and shining metal, thy head is of azure blue, and the brilliance of the turquoise encircleth thee. O thou god An, who hast had existence for millions of years, who pervadest all things with thy body, who art beautiful in countenance in the Land of Holiness (*i.e.*, the underworld), grant thou to me splendour in heaven, might upon earth, and triumph in the underworld. Grant thou that I may sail down to Tattu like a living soul, and up to Abtu like the phœnix; and grant that I may enter in and come forth from the pylons of the lands of the underworld without let or hindrance. May loaves of bread be given unto me in the house of coolness, and offerings of food and drink in Annu (Heliopolis), and a homestead for ever and for ever in the Field of Reeds[2] with wheat and barley therefor."

---

[1] A name of Osiris.
[2] A division of the "Fields of Peace" or Elysian Fields.

In the long and important hymn in the Papyrus of Hunefer[1] occurs the following petition, which is put into the mouth of the deceased:—

"Grant that I may follow in the train of thy Majesty even as I did upon earth. Let my soul be called [into the presence], and let it be found by the side of the lords of right and truth. I have come into the City of God, the region which existed in primeval time, with [my] soul, and with [my] double, and with [my] translucent form, to dwell in this land. The God thereof is the lord of right and truth, he is the lord of the *tchefau* food of the gods, and he is most holy. His land draweth unto itself every land; the South cometh sailing down the river thereto, and the North, steered thither by winds, cometh daily to make festival therein according to the command of the God thereof, who is the Lord of peace therein. And doth he not say, 'The happiness thereof is a care unto me'? The god who dwelleth therein worketh right and truth; unto him that doeth these things he giveth old age, and to him that followeth after them rank and honour, until at length he attaineth unto a happy funeral and burial in the Holy Land" (*i.e.*, the underworld).

The deceased, having recited these words of prayer and adoration to Rā, the symbol of Almighty God, and to his son Osiris, next "cometh forth into the Hall of Maāti, that he may be separated from every sin which

[1] See *The Chapters of Coming Forth by Day*, pp. 343-346.

he hath done, and may behold the faces of the gods."[1] From the earliest times the Maāti were the two goddesses Isis and Nephthys, and they were so called because they represented the ideas of straightness, integrity, righteousness, what is right, the truth, and such like; the word Maāt originally meant a measuring reed or stick. They were supposed either to sit in the Hall of Maāt outside the shrine of Osiris, or to stand by the side of this god in the shrine; an example of the former position will be seen in the Papyrus of Ani (Plate 31), and of the latter in the Papyrus of Hunefer (Plate 4). The original idea of the Hall of Maāt or Maāti was that it contained forty-two gods, a fact which we may see from the following passage in the Introduction to Chapter CXXV. of the Book of the Dead. The deceased says to Osiris:—

"Homage to thee, O thou great God, thou Lord of the two Maāt goddesses! I have come to thee, O my Lord, and I have made myself to come hither that I may behold thy beauties. I know thee, and I know thy name, and I know the names of the two and forty gods who live with thee in this Hall of Maāti, who live as watchers of sinners and who feed upon their blood on that day when the characters (*or* lives) of men are reckoned up (*or* taken into account) in the presence of the god Un-nefer. Verily, God of the Rekhti-Merti

[1] This quotation is from the title of Chapter CXXV. of the Book of the Dead.

THE FORTY-TWO GODS. 127

(*i.e.*, the twin sisters of the two eyes), the Lord of the city of Maâti is thy name. Verily I have come to thee, and I have brought Maât unto thee, and I have destroyed wickedness."

The deceased then goes on to enumerate the sins or offences which he has not committed, and he concludes by saying "I am pure; I am pure; I am pure; I am pure. My purity is the purity of the great Bennu which is in the city of Suten-henen (Heracleopolis), for, behold, I am the nostrils of the God of breath, who maketh all mankind to live on the day when the Eye of Râ is full in Annu (Heliopolis) at the end of the second month of the season PERT.[1] I have seen the Eye of Râ when it was full in Annu;[2] therefore let not evil befall me either in this land or in this Hall of Maâti, because I, even I, know the names of the gods who are therein."

Now as the gods who live in the Hall of Maât with Osiris are two and forty in number, we should expect that two and forty sins or offences would be mentioned in the addresses which the deceased makes to them; but this is not the case, for the sins enumerated in the Introduction never reach this number. In the great illustrated papyri of the XVIIIth and XIXth dynasties we find, however, that notwithstanding the fact that

---

[1] *I.e.*, the last day of the sixth month of the Egyptian year, called by the Copts Mekhir.
[2] The allusion here seems to be to the Summer *or* Winter Solstice.

a large number of sins, which the deceased declares he has not committed, are mentioned in the Introduction, the scribes and artists added a series of negative statements, forty-two in number, which they set out in a tabular form. This, clearly, is an attempt to make the sins mentioned equal in number to the gods of the Hall of Maāt, and it would seem as if they preferred to compose an entirely new form of this section of the one hundred and twenty-fifth chapter to making any attempt to add to or alter the older section. The artists, then, depicted a Hall of Maāt, the doors of which are wide open, and the cornice of which is formed of uraei and feathers, symbolic of Maāt. Over the middle of the cornice is a seated deity with hands extended, the right over the Eye of Horus, and the left over a pool. At the end of the Hall are seated the goddesses of Maāt, *i.e.*, Isis and Nephthys, the deceased adoring Osiris who is seated on a throne, a balance with the heart of the deceased in one scale, and the feather, symbolic of Maāt, in the other, and Thoth painting a large feather. In this Hall sit the forty-two gods, and as the deceased passes by each, the deceased addresses him by his name and at the same time declares that he has not committed a certain sin. An examination of the different papyri shows that the scribes often made mistakes in writing this list of gods and list of sins, and, as the result, the deceased is made to recite before one god the confession which strictly belongs to another. Inasmuch as the deceased always says after pronouncing the name of each god, "I have not done" such and such a sin, the whole group of addresses has been called the "Negative Confession." The fundamental ideas of religion and morality which underlie this Confession are exceedingly old, and we may gather from it with tolerable clearness what the ancient Egyptian believed to constitute his duty towards God and towards his neighbour.

It is impossible to explain the fact that forty-two gods only are addressed, and equally so to say why this number was adopted. Some have believed that the forty-two gods represented each a nome of Egypt, and much support is given to this view by the fact that most of the lists of nomes make the number to be forty-two; but then, again, the lists do not agree. The classical authors differ also, for by some of these writers the nomes are said to be thirty-six in number, and by others forty-six are enumerated. These differences may, however, be easily explained, for the central administration may at any time have added to or taken from the number of nomes for fiscal or other considerations, and we shall probably be correct in assuming that at the time the Negative Confession was drawn up in the tabular form in which we meet it in the XVIIIth dynasty the nomes were forty-two in number. Support is also lent to this view by the fact that the earliest form of the Confession, which forms the

K

Introduction to Chapter CXXV., mentions less than forty sins. Incidentally we may notice that the forty-two gods are subservient to Osiris, and that they only occupy a subordinate position in the Hall of Judgment, for it is the result of the weighing of the heart of the deceased in the balance that decides his future. Before passing to the description of the Hall of Judgment where the balance is set, it is necessary to give a rendering of the Negative Confession which, presumably, the deceased recites before his heart is weighed in the balance; it is made from the Papyrus of Nu.[1]

1. "Hail Usekh-nemtet (*i.e.*, Long of strides), who comest forth from Annu (Heliopolis), I have not done iniquity.

2. "Hail Hept-seshet (*i.e.*, Embraced by flame), who comest forth from Kher-āba,[2] I have not robbed with violence.

3. "Hail Fenti (*i.e.*, Nose), who comest forth from Khemennu (Hermopolis), I have not done violence to any man.

4. "Hail Ām-khaibitu (*i.e.*, Eater of shades), who comest forth from the Qereret (*i.e.*, the cavern where the Nile rises), I have not committed theft.

5. "Hail Neha-hra (*i.e.*, Stinking face), who comest forth from Restau, I have slain neither man nor woman.

6. "Hail Bereti (*i.e.*, Double Lion-god), who comest forth from heaven, I have not made light the bushel.

---
[1] British Museum, No. 10,477.   [2] A city near Memphis.

7. "Hail Maata-f-em-seshet (*i.e.*, Fiery eyes), who comest forth from Sekhem (Letopolis), I have not acted deceitfully.

8. "Hail Neba (*i.e.*, Flame), who comest forth and retreatest, I have not purloined the things which belong unto God.

9. "Hail Set-qesu (*i.e.*, Crusher of bones), who comest forth from Suten-henen (Heracleopolis), I have not uttered falsehood.

10. "Hail Khemi (*i.e.*, Overthrower), who comest forth from Shetait (*i.e.*, the hidden place), I have not carried off goods by force.

11. "Hail Uatch-nesert (*i.e.*, Vigorous of Flame), who comest forth from Het-ka-Ptah (Memphis), I have not uttered vile (*or* evil) words.

12. "Hail Hra-f-ha-f (*i.e.*, He whose face is behind him), who comest forth from the cavern and the deep, I have not carried off food by force.

13. "Hail Qerti (*i.e.*, the double Nile source), who comest forth from the Underworld, I have not acted deceitfully.

14. "Hail Ta-ret (*i.e.*, Fiery-foot), who comest forth out of the darkness, I have not eaten my heart (*i.e.* lost my temper and become angry).

15. "Hail Hetch-abehu (*i.e.*, Shining teeth), who comest forth from Ta-she (*i.e.*, the Fayyûm), I have invaded no [man's land].

16. "Hail Ām-senef (*i.e.*, Eater of blood), who comest

forth from the house of the block, I have not slaughtered animals which are the possessions of God.

17. "Hail Ām-besek (*i.e.*, Eater of entrails), who comest forth from Mābet, I have not laid waste the lands which have been ploughed.

18. "Hail Neb-Maāt (*i.e.*, Lord of Maāt), who comest forth from the city of the two Maāti, I have not pried into matters to make mischief.

19. "Hail Thenemi (*i.e.*, Retreater), who comest forth from Bast (*i.e.*, Bubastis), I have not set my mouth in motion against any man.

20. "Hail Ānti, who comest forth from Annu (Heliopolis), I have not given way to wrath without due cause.

21. "Hail Tututef, who comest forth from the nome of Ati, I have not committed fornication, and I have not committed sodomy.

22. "Hail Uamemti, who comest forth from the house of slaughter, I have not polluted myself.

23. "Hail Maa-ant-f (*i.e.*, Seer of what is brought to him), who comest forth from the house of the god Amsu, I have not lain with the wife of a man.

24. "Hail Her-seru, who comest forth from Nehatu, I have not made any man to be afraid.

25. "Hail Neb-Sekhem, who comest forth from the Lake of Kaui, I have not made my speech to burn with anger.[1]

---

[1] Literally, "I have not been hot of mouth."

26. "Hail Seshet-kheru (*i.e.*, Orderer of speech), who comest forth from Urit, I have not made myself deaf unto the words of right and truth.

27. "Hail Nekhen (*i.e.*, Babe), who comest forth from the Lake of Heqāt, I have not made another person to weep.

28. "Hail Kenemti, who comest forth from Kenemet, I have not uttered blasphemies.

29. "Hail An-hetep-f (*i.e.*, Bringer of his offering), who comest forth from Sau, I have not acted with violence.

30. "Hail Ser-kheru (*i.e.*, Disposer of Speech), who comest forth from Unsi, I have not hastened my heart.[1]

31. "Hail Neb-hrau (*i.e.*, Lord of Faces), who comest forth from Netchefet, I have not pierced (?) my skin (?), and I have not taken vengeance on the god.

32. "Hail Serekhi, who comest forth from Uthent, I have not multiplied my speech beyond what should be said.

33. "Hail Neb-ābui (*i.e.*, Lord of horns), who comest forth from Sauti, I have not committed fraud, [and I have not] looked upon evil.

34. "Hail Nefer-Tem, who comest forth from Ptah-het-ka (Memphis), I have never uttered curses against the king.

35. "Hail Tem-sep, who comest forth from Tattu, I have not fouled running water.

---

[1] *I e.*, acted without due consideration.

36. "Hail Ari-em-ab-f, who comest forth from Tebti, I have not exalted my speech.

37. "Hail Ahi, who comest forth from Nu, I have not uttered curses against God.

38. "Hail Uatch-rekhit [who comest forth from his shrine (?)], I have not behaved with insolence.

39. "Hail Neheb-nefert, who comest forth from his temple, I have not made distinctions.[1]

40. "Hail Neheb-kau, who comest forth from thy cavern, I have not increased my wealth except by means of such things as are mine own possessions.

41. "Hail Tcheser-tep, who comest forth from thy shrine, I have not uttered curses against that which belongeth to God and is with me.

42. "Hail An-ā-f (*i.e.*, Bringer of his arm), [who comest forth from Ankert], I have not thought scorn of the god of the city."

A brief examination of this "Confession" shows that the Egyptian code of morality was very comprehensive, and it would be very hard to find an act, the commission of which would be reckoned a sin when the "Confession" was put together, which is not included under one or other part of it. The renderings of the words for certain sins are not always definite or exact, because we do not know the precise idea which the framer of this remarkable document had. The deceased states that he has neither cursed God, nor thought scorn

[1] *I.e.*, I have not been guilty of favouritism.

of the god of his city, nor cursed the king, nor committed theft of any kind, nor murder, nor adultery, nor sodomy, nor crimes against the god of generation; he has not been imperious or haughty, or violent, or wrathful, or hasty in deed, or a hypocrite, or an accepter of persons, or a blasphemer, or crafty, or avaricious, or fraudulent, or deaf to pious words, or a party to evil actions, or proud, or puffed up; he has terrified no man, he has not cheated in the market-place, and he has neither fouled the public watercourse nor laid waste the tilled land of the community. This is, in brief, the confession which the deceased makes; and the next act in the Judgment Scene is weighing the heart of the deceased in the scales. As none of the oldest papyri of the Book of the Dead supplies us with a representation of this scene, we must have recourse to the best of the illustrated papyri of the latter half of the XVIIIth and of the XIXth dynasties. The details of the Judgment Scene vary greatly in various papyri, but the essential parts of it are always preserved. The following is the description of the judgment of Ani, as it appears in his wonderful papyrus preserved in the British Museum.

In the underworld, and in that portion of it which is called the Hall of Maāti, is set a balance wherein the heart of the deceased is to be weighed. The beam is suspended by a ring upon a projection from the standard of the balance made in the form of the feather which is the symbol of Maāt, or what is right and true. The tongue of the balance is fixed to the beam, and when this is exactly level, the tongue is as straight as the standard; if either end of the beam inclines downwards the tongue cannot remain in a perpendicular position. It must be distinctly understood that the heart which was weighed in the one scale was not expected to make the weight which was in the other to kick the beam, for all that was asked or required of the deceased was that his heart should balance exactly the symbol of the law. The standard was sometimes surmounted by a human head wearing the feather of Maāt; sometimes by the head of a jackal, the animal sacred to Anubis; and sometimes by the head of an ibis, the bird sacred to Thoth; in the Papyrus of Ani a dog-headed ape, the associate of Thoth, sits on the top of the standard. In some papyri (*e.g.*, those of Ani [1] and Hunefer [2]), in addition to Osiris, the king of the underworld and judge of the dead, the gods of his cycle or company appear as witnesses of the judgment. In the Papyrus of the priestess Anhai [3] in the British Museum the great and the little companies of the gods appear as witnesses, but the artist was so careless that instead of nine gods in each group he painted six in one and five in the other. In the Turin papyrus [4] we see the whole of the forty-two gods, to whom the deceased recited the

---

[1] About B.C. 1500. [2] About B.C. 1370. [3] About B.C. 1000.
[4] Written in the Ptolemaic period.

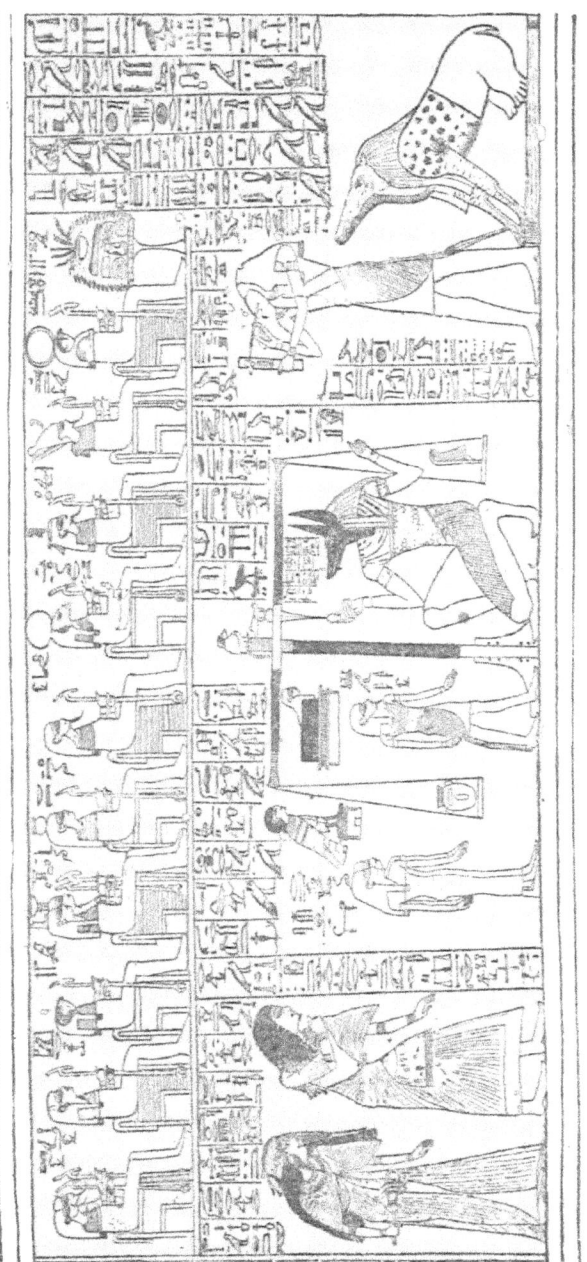

The weighing of the heart of the scribe Ani in the Balance in the presence of the gods.

THE GODS IN JUDGMENT. 139

"Negative Confession," seated in the judgment-hall. The gods present at the weighing of Ani's heart are—

1. RĀ-HARMACHIS, hawk-headed, the Sun-god of the dawn and of noon.
2. TEMU, the Sun-god of the evening, the great god of Heliopolis. He is depicted always in human form and with the face of a man, a fact which proves that he had at a very early period passed through all the forms in which gods are represented, and had arrived at that of a man. He has upon his head the crowns of the South and North.
3. SHU, man-headed, the son of Rā and Hathor, the personification of the sunlight.
4. TEFNUT, lion-headed, the twin-sister of Shu, the personification of moisture.
5. SEB, man-headed, the son of Shu, the personification of the earth.
6. NUT, woman-headed, the female counterpart of the gods Nu and Seb; she was the personification of the primeval water, and later of the sky.
7. ISIS, woman-headed, the sister-wife of Osiris, and mother of Horus.
8. NEPHTHYS, woman-headed, the sister-wife of Osiris, and mother of Anubis.
9. HORUS, the "great god," hawk-headed, whose worship was probably the oldest in Egypt.
10. HATHOR, woman-headed, the personification of that portion of the sky where the sun rose and set.

11. Hu, man-headed, and

12. Sa, also man-headed; these gods are present in the boat of Rā in the scenes which depict the creation.

On one side of the balance kneels the god Anubis, jackal-headed, who holds the weight of the tongue of the balance in his right hand, and behind him stands Thoth, the scribe of the gods, ibis-headed, holding in his hands a reed wherewith to write down the result of the weighing. Near him is seated the tri-formed beast Ām-mit, the "Eater of the Dead," who waits to devour the heart of Ani should it be found to be light. In the Papyrus of Neb-qet at Paris this beast is seen lying by the side of a lake of fire, at each corner of which is seated a dog-headed ape; this lake is also seen in Chapter CXXVI. of the Book of the Dead. The gods who are seated before a table of offerings, and Anubis, and Thoth, and Ām-mit, are the beings who conduct the case, so to speak, against Ani. On the other side of the balance stand Ani and his wife Thuthu with their heads reverently bent; they are depicted in human form, and wear garments and ornaments similar to those which they wore upon earth. His soul, in the form of a man-headed hawk standing upon a pylon, is present, also a man-headed, rectangular object, resting upon a pylon, which has frequently been supposed to represent the deceased in an embryonic state. In the Papyrus of Anhai two of these objects appear, one on each side of the balance; they are described as Shai and Renenet, two words which are translated by "Destiny" and "Fortune" respectively. It is most probable, as the reading of the name of the object is *Meskhenet*, and as the deity Meskhenet represents sometimes both Shai and Renenet, that the artist intended the object to represent both deities, even though we find the god Shai standing below it close to the standard of the balance. Close by the soul stand two goddesses called Meskhenet and Renenet respectively; the former is, probably, one of the four goddesses who assisted at the resurrection of Osiris, and the latter the personification of Fortune, which has already been included under the *Meskhenet* object above, the personification of Destiny.

It will be remembered that Meskhenet accompanied Isis, Nephthys, Heqet, and Khnemu to the house of the lady Rut-Tettet, who was about to bring forth three children. When these deities arrived, having changed their forms into those of women, they found Rā-user standing there. And when they had made music for him, he said to them, "Mistresses, there is a woman in travail here;" and they replied, "Let us see her, for we know how to deliver a woman." Rā-user then brought them into the house, and the goddesses shut themselves in with the lady Rut-Tettet. Isis took her place before her, and Nephthys behind her, whilst Heqet hastened the birth of the children; as each child was born Meskhenet stepped up to him and said, "A king who shall have dominion over the whole land," and the god Khnemu bestowed health upon his limbs.[1] Of these five gods, Isis, Nephthys, Meskhenet, Heqet, and Khnemu, the first three are present at the judgment of Ani; Khnemu is mentioned in Ani's address to his heart (see below), and only Heqet is unrepresented.

As the weighing of his heart is about to take place Ani says, "My heart, my mother! My heart, my mother! My heart whereby I came into being! May naught stand up to oppose me in the judgment; may there be no opposition to me in the presence of the sovereign princes; may there be no parting of thee from me in the presence of him that keepeth the Balance! Thou art my *ka*, the dweller in my body; the god Khnemu who knitteth and strengtheneth my limbs. Mayest thou come forth into the place of happiness whither we go. May the princes of the court of Osiris, who order the circumstances of the lives of men, not cause my name to stink." Some papyri add, "Let it be satisfactory unto us, and let the listening be satisfactory unto us, and let there be joy of heart unto us at the weighing of words. Let not that which is false be uttered against me before the great god, the lord of Amentet! Verily how great shalt thou be when thou risest in triumph!"

The tongue of the balance having been examined

[1] See Erman, *Westcar Papyrus*, Berlin, 1890, hieroglyphic transcript, plates 9 and 10.

THE SPEECH OF THOTH.

by Anubis, and the ape having indicated to his associate Thoth that the beam is exactly straight, and that the heart, therefore, counterbalances the feather symbolic of Maāt (*i.e.*, right, truth, law, etc.), neither outweighing nor underweighing it, Thoth writes down the result, and then makes the following address to the gods :—

"Hear ye this judgment. The heart of Osiris hath in very truth been weighed, and his soul hath stood as a witness for him; it hath been found true by trial in the Great Balance. There hath not been found any wickedness in him; he hath not wasted the offerings in the temples; he hath not done harm by his deeds; and he spread abroad no evil reports while he was upon earth."

In answer to this report the company of the gods, who are styled "the great company of the gods," reply, "That which cometh forth from thy mouth, O Thoth, who dwellest in Khemennu (Hermopolis), is confirmed. Osiris, the scribe Ani, triumphant, is holy and righteous. He hath not sinned, neither hath he done evil against us. The Devourer Ām-mit shall not be allowed to prevail over him, and meat-offerings and entrance into the presence of the god Osiris shall be granted unto him, together with a homestead for ever in the Field of Peace, as unto the followers of Horus."[1]

[1] These are a class of mythological beings, or demi-gods, who already in the Vth dynasty were supposed to recite prayers on behalf of the deceased, and to assist Horus and Set in performing funeral ceremonies. See my *Papyrus of Ani*, p. cxxv.

Here we notice at once that the deceased is identified with Osiris, the god and judge of the dead, and that they have bestowed upon him the god's own name; the reason of this is as follows. The friends of the deceased performed for him all the ceremonies and rites which were performed for Osiris by Isis and Nephthys, and it was assumed that, as a result, the same things which took place in favour of Osiris would also happen on behalf of the deceased, and that in fact, the deceased would become the counterpart of Osiris. Everywhere in the texts of the Book of the Dead the deceased is identified with Osiris, from B.C. 3400 to the Roman period. Another point to notice is the application of the words *maā kheru* to the deceased, a term which I have, for want of a better word, rendered "triumphant." These words actually mean "true of voice" or "right of word," and indicate that the person to whom they are applied has acquired the power of using his voice in such a way that when the invisible beings are addressed by him they will render unto him all the service which he has obtained the right to demand. It is well known that in ancient times magicians and sorcerers were wont to address spirits or demons in a peculiar tone of voice, and that all magical formulæ were recited in a similar manner; the use of the wrong sound or tone of voice would result in the most disastrous consequences to the speaker, and perhaps in death. The deceased had

WORDS OF POWER. 145

to make his way through a number of regions in the underworld, and to pass through many series of halls, the doors of which were guarded by beings who were prepared, unless properly addressed, to be hostile to the new-comer; he also had need to take passage in a boat, and to obtain the help of the gods and of the powers of the various localities wherein he wanted to travel if he wished to pass safely into the place where he would be. The Book of the Dead provided him with all the texts and formulæ which he would have to recite to secure this result, but unless the words contained in them were pronounced in a proper manner, and said in a proper tone of voice, they would have no effect upon the powers of the underworld. The term *maā kheru* is applied but very rarely to the living, but commonly to the dead, and indeed the dead needed most the power which these words indicated. In the case of Ani, the gods, having accepted the favourable report of the result obtained by weighing Ani's heart by Thoth, style him *maā kheru*, which is equivalent to conferring upon him power to overcome all opposition, of every kind, which he may meet. Henceforth every door will open at his command, every god will hasten to obey immediately Ani has uttered his name, and those whose duty it is to provide celestial food for the beatified will do so for him when once the order has been given. Before passing on to other matters it is interesting to note that the term *maā kheru* is not applied to **Ani** by himself in the Judgment Scene, nor by Thoth, the scribe of the gods, nor by Horus when he introduces him to Osiris; it is only the gods who can make a man *maā kheru*, and thereby he also escapes from the Devourer.

The judgment ended, Horus, the son of Isis, who has assumed all the attributes of his father Osiris, takes Ani's left hand in his right and leads him up to the shrine wherein the god Osiris is seated. The god wears the white crown with feathers, and he holds in his hands a sceptre, a crook, and whip, or flail, which typify sovereignty and dominion. His throne is a tomb, of which the bolted doors and the cornice of uraei may be seen painted on the side. At the back of his neck hangs the *menat* or symbol of joy and happiness; on his right hand stands Nephthys, and on his left stands Isis. Before him, standing on a lotus flower, are the four children of Horus, Mestha, Hāpi, Tuamutef, and Qebhsennuf, who presided over and protected the intestines of the dead; close by hangs the skin of a bull with which magical ideas seem to have been associated. The top of the shrine in which the god sits is surmounted by uraei, wearing disks on their heads, and the cornice also is similarly decorated. In several papyri the god is seen standing up in the shrine, sometimes with and sometimes without the goddesses Isis and Nephthys. In the Papyrus of **Hunefer** we find a most interesting variant of this

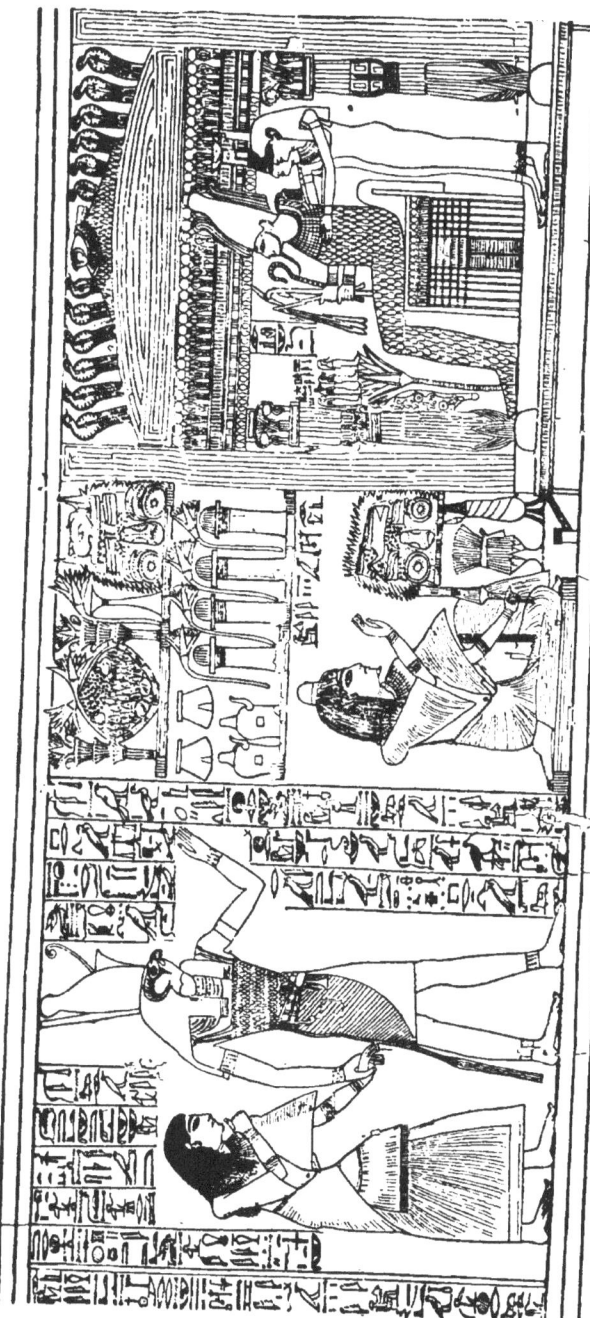

Horus, the son of Isis, leading the scribe Ani into the presence of Osiris, the god and judge of the dead; before the shrine of the god Ani kneels in adoration and presents offerings.

portion of the scene, for the throne of Osiris rests upon, or in, water. This reminds us of the passage in the one hundred and twenty-sixth chapter of the Book of the Dead in which the god Thoth says to the deceased, "Who is he whose roof is of fire, whose walls are living uraei, and the floor of whose house is a stream of running water? Who is he, I say?" The deceased answers, "It is Osiris," and the god says, "Come forward, then; for verily thou shalt be mentioned [to him]."

When Horus had led in Ani he addressed Osiris, saying, "I have come unto thee, O Un-nefer, and I have brought the Osiris Ani unto thee. His heart hath been found righteous and it hath come forth from the balance; it hath not sinned against any god or any goddess. Thoth hath weighed it according to the decree uttered unto him by the company of the gods; and it is very true and right. Grant unto him cakes and ale; and let him enter into thy presence; and may he be like unto the followers of Horus for ever!" After this address Ani, kneeling by the side of tables of offerings of fruit, flowers, etc., which he has brought unto Osiris, says, "O Lord of Amentet, I am in thy presence. There is no sin in me, I have not lied wittingly, nor have I done aught with a false heart. Grant that I may be like unto those favoured ones who are round about thee, and that I may be an Osiris greatly favoured of the beautiful god and beloved of the Lord of the world, [I], the royal scribe of Maāt, who loveth him, Ani, triumphant before Osiris."[1] Thus we come to the end of the scene of the weighing of the heart.

The man who has passed safely through this ordeal has now to meet the gods of the underworld, and the Book of the Dead provides the words which "the heart which is righteous and sinless" shall say unto them. One of the fullest and most correct texts of "the speech of the deceased when he cometh forth true of voice from the Hall of the Maāti goddesses" is found in the Papyrus of Nu; in it the deceased says:—

"Homage to you, O ye gods who dwell in the Hall of the Maāti goddesses, I, even I, know you, and I know your names. Let me not fall under your knives of slaughter, and bring ye not forward my wickedness unto the god in whose train ye are; and let not evil hap come upon me by your means. O declare ye me true of voice in the presence of Neb-er-tcher, because I have done that which is right and true in Ta-mera (*i.e.*, Egypt). I have not cursed God, therefore let not evil hap come upon me through the King who dwelleth in his day.

"Homage to you, O ye gods, who dwell in the Hall of the Maāti goddesses, who are without evil in your

---

[1] Or "true of voice in respect of Osiris;" *i.e.*, Ani makes his petition, and Osiris is to hear and answer because he has uttered the right words in the right manner, and in the right tone of voice.

bodies, and who live upon right and truth, and who feed yourselves upon right and truth in the presence of the god Horus, who dwelleth in his divine Disk; deliver ye me from the god Baba[1] who feedeth upon the entrails of the mighty ones upon the day of the great reckoning. O grant ye that I may come to you, for I have not committed faults, I have not sinned, I have not done evil, I have not borne false witness; therefore let nothing [evil] be done unto me. I live upon right and truth, and I feed upon right and truth. I have performed the commandments of men [as well as] the things whereat are gratified the gods; I have made God to be at peace [with me by doing] that which is his will. I have given bread to the hungry man, and water to the thirsty man, and apparel to the naked man, and a boat to the [shipwrecked] mariner. I have made holy offerings to the gods, and sepulchral meals to the beatified dead. Be ye then my deliverers, be ye then my protectors, and make ye not accusation against me in the presence of [Osiris]. I am clean of mouth and clean of hands; therefore let it be said unto me by those who shall behold me, 'Come in peace, come in peace.' I have heard the mighty word which the spiritual bodies spake unto the Cat[2] in the house

---

[1] The firstborn son of Osiris.
[2] *I.e.*, Rā as the slayer of the serpent of darkness, the head of which he cuts off with a knife. (See above, p. 63). The usual reading is "which the Ass spake to the Cat;" the Ass being Osiris and the Cat Rā.

of Hapt-re. I have testified in the presence of Hra-f-ha-f, and he hath given [his] decision. I have seen the things over which the Persea tree spreadeth within Re-stau. I am he who hath offered up prayers to the gods and who knoweth their persons. I have come, and I have advanced to make the declaration of right and truth, and to set the Balance upon what supporteth it in the region of Ankert.

"Hail, thou who art exalted upon thy standard (*i.e.*, Osiris), thou lord of the 'Atefu' crown whose name is proclaimed as 'Lord of the winds,' deliver thou me from thy divine messengers who cause dire deeds to happen, and who cause calamities to come into being, and who are without coverings for their faces, for I have done that which is right and true for the Lord of right and truth. I have purified myself and my breast with libations, and my hinder parts with the things which make clean, and my inward parts have been [immersed] in the Pool of Right and Truth. There is no single member of mine which lacketh right and truth. I have been purified in the Pool of the South, and I have rested in the City of the North, which is in the Field of the Grasshoppers, wherein the divine sailors of Rā bathe at the second hour of the night and at the third hour of the day; and the hearts of the gods are gratified after they have passed through it, whether it be by night, or whether it be by day. And I would that they should say unto me, 'Come forward,' and 'Who art thou?' and 'What is thy name?' These are the words which I would have the gods say unto me. [Then would I reply] 'My name is He who is provided with flowers, and Dweller in his olive tree.' Then let them say unto me straightway, 'Pass on,' and I would pass on to the city to the north of the Olive tree. 'What then wilt thou see there?' [say they. And I say] 'The Leg and the Thigh.' 'What wouldst thou say unto them?' [say they.] 'Let me see rejoicings in the land of the Fenkhu' [I reply]. 'What will they give thee? [say they]. 'A fiery flame and a crystal tablet' [I reply]. 'What wilt thou do therewith?' [say they]. 'Bury them by the furrow of Māāat as Things for the night' [I reply]. 'What wilt thou find by the furrow of Māāat?' [say they]. 'A sceptre of flint called Giver of Air' [I reply]. 'What wilt thou do with the fiery flame and the crystal tablet after thou hast buried them?' [say they]. 'I will recite words over them in the furrow. I will extinguish the fire, and I will break the tablet, and I will make a pool of water' [I reply]. Then let the gods say unto me, 'Come and enter in through the door of this Hall of the Maāti goddesses, for thou knowest us.'"

After these remarkable prayers follows a dialogue between each part of the Hall of Maāti and the deceased, which reads as follows:—

Door bolts. "We will not let thee enter in through us unless thou tellest our names."

Deceased. "'Tongue of the place of Right and Truth' is your name."

Right post. "I will not let thee enter in by me unless thou tellest my name."

Deceased. "'Scale of the lifter up of right and truth' is thy name."

Left post. "I will not let thee enter in by me unless thou tellest my name."

Deceased. "'Scale of wine' is thy name."

Threshold. "I will not let thee pass over me unless thou tellest my name."

Deceased. "'Ox of the god Seb' is thy name."

Hasp. "I will not open unto thee unless thou tellest my name."

Deceased. "'Leg-bone of his mother' is thy name."

Socket-hole. "I will not open unto thee unless thou tellest my name."

Deceased. "'Living Eye of Sebek, the lord of Bakhau,' is thy name."

Porter. "I will not open unto thee unless thou tellest my name."

Deceased. "'Elbow of the god Shu when he placeth himself to protect Osiris' is thy name."

Side posts. "We will not let thee pass in by us, unless thou tellest our names."

Deceased. "'Children of the uraei-goddesses' is your name."

"Thou knowest us; pass on, therefore, by us" [say these].

THE KNOWING OF NAMES.

Floor. "I will not let thee tread upon me, because I am silent and I am holy, and because I do not know the names of thy feet wherewith thou wouldst walk upon me; therefore tell them to me."

Deceased. "'Traveller of the god Khas' is the name of my right foot, and 'Staff of the goddess Hathor' is the name of my left foot."

"Thou knowest me; pass on, therefore, over me" [it saith].

Doorkeeper. "I will not take in thy name unless thou tellest my name."

Deceased. "'Discerner of hearts and searcher of the reins' is thy name."

Doorkeeper. "Who is the god that dwelleth in his hour? Utter his name."

Deceased. "'Māau-Taui' is his name."

Doorkeeper. "And who is Māau-Taui?"

Deceased. "He is Thoth."

Thoth. "Come! But why hast thou come?"

Deceased. "I have come and I press forward that my name may be mentioned."

Thoth. "In what state art thou?"

Deceased. "I am purified from evil things, and I am protected from the baleful deeds of those who live in their days; and I am not of them."

Thoth. "Now will I make mention of thy name [to the god]. And who is he whose roof is of fire, whose walls are living uraei, and the floor of whose house is a stream of water? Who is he, I say?"

Deceased. "It is Osiris."

Thoth. "Come forward, then; verily, mention of thy name shall be made unto him. Thy cakes [shall come] from the Eye of Rā; and thine ale [shall come] from the Eye of Rā; and thy sepulchral meals upon earth [shall come] from the Eye of Rā."

With these words Chapter CXXV comes to an end. We have seen how the deceased has passed through the ordeal of the judgment, and how the scribes provided him with hymns and prayers, and with the words of a confession with a view of facilitating his passage through the dread Hall of the Maāti goddesses. Unfortunately the answer which the god Osiris may be supposed to have made to his son Horus in respect of the deceased is not recorded, but there is no doubt that the Egyptian assumed that it would be favourable to him, and that permission would be accorded him to enter into each and every portion of the underworld, and to partake of all the delights which the beatified enjoyed under the rule of Rā and Osiris.

CHAPTER V.

THE RESURRECTION AND IMMORTALITY.

IN perusing the literature of the ancient Egyptians one of the first things which forces itself upon the mind of the reader is the frequency of allusions to the future life or to things which appertain thereto. The writers of the various religious and other works, belonging to all periods of Egyptian history, which have come down to us, tacitly assume throughout that those who once have lived in this world have "renewed" their life in that which is beyond the grave, and that they still live and will live until time shall be no more. The Egyptian belief in the existence of Almighty God is old, so old that we must seek for its beginnings in pre-dynastic times; but the belief in a future life is very much older, and its beginnings must be as old, at least, as the oldest human remains which have been found in Egypt. To attempt to measure by years the remoteness of the period when these were committed to the earth is futile, for no date that could be given them is likely to be even approximately correct, and they may as well date from B.C. 12,000 as from B.C. 8000. Of one fact, however, we may be quite certain; that is to say, that the oldest human remains that have been found in Egypt bear upon them traces of the use of bitumen, which proves that the Egyptians at the very beginning of their stay in the valley of the Nile made some attempt to preserve their dead by means of mummification.[1] If they were, as many think, invaders who had made their way across Arabia and the Red Sea and the eastern desert of the Nile, they may have brought the idea and habit of preserving their dead with them, or they may have adopted, in a modified form, some practice in use among the aboriginal inhabitants whom they found on their arrival in Egypt; in either case the fact that they attempted to preserve their dead by the use of substances which would arrest decay is certain, and in a degree their attempt has succeeded.

The existence of the non-historic inhabitants of Egypt has been revealed to us in recent years by means of a number of successful excavations which have been made in Upper Egypt on both sides of the Nile by several European and native explorers, and one of the most striking results has been the discovery of three different kinds of burials, which undoubtedly belong to three different periods, as we may see by examining the various objects which have been found in the early graves at Nakâdah and other non-historic sites of the

---

[1] See J. de Morgan, *Ethnographie Préhistorique*, Paris, 1897, p. 139.

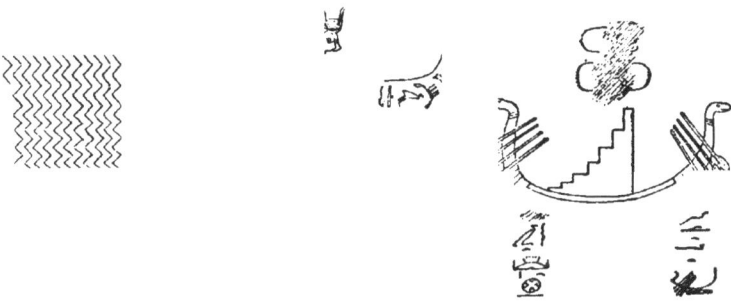

The Elysian Fields of the Egyptians according to the Papyrus of Nebseni (XVIIIth dynasty

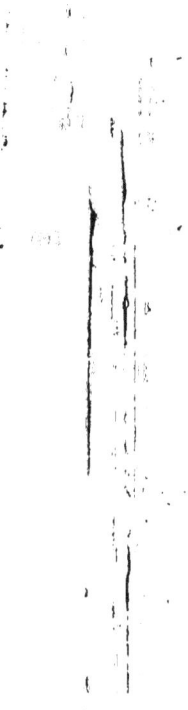

same age and type. In the oldest tombs we find the skeleton laid upon its left side, with the limbs bent: the knees are on a level with the breast, and the hands are placed in front of the face. Generally the head faces towards the south, but no invariable rule seems to have been observed as to its "orientation." Before the body was laid in the ground it was either wrapped in gazelle skin or laid in loose grass; the substance used for the purposes of wrapping probably depended upon the social condition of the deceased. In burials of this class there are no traces of mummification, or of burning, or of stripping the flesh from the bones. In the next oldest graves the bodies are found to have been wholly or partly stripped of their flesh; in the former case all the bones are found cast indiscriminately in the grave, in the latter the bones of the hands and the feet were laid together, while the rest of the skeleton is scattered about in wild confusion. Graves of this period are found to be oriented either north or south, and the bodies in them usually have the head separated from the body; sometimes it is clear that the bodies have been "jointed" so that they might occupy less space. Occasionally the bodies are found lying upon their backs with their legs and arms folded over them; in this case they are covered over with clay casings. In certain graves it is clear that the body has been burnt. Now in all classes of tombs belonging to the prehistoric period in Egypt we find offerings in vases and vessels of various kinds, a fact which proves beyond all doubt that the men who made these graves believed that their dead friends and relatives would live again in some place, of the whereabouts of which they probably had very vague ideas, in a life which was, presumably, not unlike that which they had lived upon earth. The flint tools, knives, scrapers and the like indicate that they thought they would hunt and slay their quarry when brought down, and fight their foes; and the schist objects found in the graves, which M. de Morgan identifies as amulets, shows that even in those early days man believed that he could protect himself against the powers of supernatural and invisible enemies by talismans. The man who would hunt and fight in the next world must live again; and if he would live again it must be either in his old body or in a new one; if in the old body, it must be revivified. But once having imagined a new life, probably in a new body, death a second time was not, the prehistoric Egyptian hoped, within the bounds of possibility. Here, then, we have the origin of the grand ideas of the RESURRECTION and IMMORTALITY.

There is every reason for believing that the prehistoric Egyptian expected to eat, and to drink, and to lead a life of pleasure in the region where he imagined his heaven to be, and there is little doubt that he thought the body in which he would live there would be not unlike the body which he had while he was upon earth. At this stage his ideas of the supernatural and of the future life would be like those of any man of the same race who stood on the same level in the scale of civilization, but in every way he was a great contrast to the Egyptian who lived, let us say, in the time of Mena, the first historical king of Egypt, the date of whom for convenience' sake is placed at B.C. 4400. The interval between the time when the prehistoric Egyptians made the graves described above and the reign of Mena must have been very considerable, and we may justly believe it to represent some thousands of years; but whatever its length, we find that the time was not sufficient to wipe out the early views which had been handed on from generation to generation, or even to modify some of the beliefs which we now know to have existed in an almost unchanged state at the latest period of Egyptian history. In the texts which were edited by the priests of Heliopolis we find references to a state or condition of things, as far as social matters are concerned, which could only exist in a society of men who were half savages, And we see from later works, when extracts are made from the earlier texts which contain such references, that the passages in which objectionable allusions occur are either omitted altogether or modified. We know of a certainty that the educated men of the College of Heliopolis cannot have indulged in the excesses which the deceased kings for whom they

M

prepared the funeral texts are assumed to enjoy, and the mention of the nameless abomination which the savage Egyptian inflicted upon his vanquished foe can only have been allowed to remain in them because of their own reverence for the written word.

In passing it must be mentioned that the religious ideas of the men who were buried without mutilation of limbs, or stripping of flesh from the body, or burning, must have been different from those of the men who practised such things on the dead. The former are buried in the ante-natal position of a child, and we may perhaps be justified in seeing in this custom the symbol of a hope that as the child is born from this position into the world, so might the deceased be born into the life in the world beyond the grave; and the presence of amulets, the object of which was to protect the body, seems to indicate that they expected the actual body to rise again. The latter, by the mutilation of the bodies and the burning of the dead, seem to show that they had no hope of living again in their natural bodies, and how far they had approached to the conception of the resurrection of a spiritual body we shall probably never know. When we arrive at the IVth dynasty we find that, so far from any practice of mutilation or burning of the body being common, every text assumes that the body is to be buried whole; this fact indicates a reversal of the custom of mutilation or burning, which must have been in use, however, for a considerable time. It is to this reversal that we probably owe such passages as, "O flesh of Pepi, rot not, decay not, stink not;" "Pepi goeth forth with his flesh;" "thy bones shall not be destroyed, and thy flesh shall not perish,"[1] etc.; and they denote a return to the views and ways of the earliest people known to us in Egypt.

In the interval which elapsed between the period of the prehistoric burials and the IVth dynasty, the Egyptian formulated certain theories about the component parts of his own body, and we must consider these briefly before we can describe the form in which the dead were believed to rise. The physical body of a man was called KHAT, a word which indicates something in which decay is inherent; it was this which was buried in the tomb after mummification, and its preservation from destruction of every kind was the object of all amulets, magical ceremonies, prayers, and formulæ, from the earliest to the latest times. The god Osiris even possessed such a body, and its various members were preserved as relics in several shrines in Egypt. Attached to the body in some remarkable way was the KA, or "double," of a man; it may be defined as an abstract individuality or personality which was endowed with all his characteristic attributes, and it possessed an absolutely independent existence. It was free to move from

---

[1] See *Recueil de Travaux*, tom. v. pp. 55, 185 (lines 169, 347, 353).

place to place upon earth at will, and it could enter heaven and hold converse with the gods. The offerings made in the tombs at all periods were intended for the nourishment of the KA, and it was supposed to be able to eat and drink and to enjoy the odour of incense. In the earliest times a certain portion of the tomb was set apart for the use of the KA, and the religious organization of the period ordered that a class of priests should perform ceremonies and recite prayers at stated seasons for the benefit of the KA in the KA-chapel; these men were known as "KA priests." In the period when the pyramids were built it was firmly believed that the deceased, in some form, was able to be purified, and to sit down and to eat bread with it "unceasingly and for ever;" and the KA who was not supplied with a sufficiency of food in the shape of offerings of bread, cakes, flowers, fruit, wine, ale, and the like, was in serious danger of starvation.

The soul was called BA, and the ideas which the Egyptians held concerning it are somewhat difficult to reconcile; the meaning of the word seems to be something like "sublime," "noble," "mighty." The BA dwelt in the KA, and seems to have had the power of becoming corporeal or incorporeal at will; it had both substance and form, and is frequently depicted on the papyri and monuments as a human-headed hawk; in nature and substance it is stated to be

THE HEART, SPIRIT AND SHADOW. 165

ethereal. It had the power to leave the tomb, and to pass up into heaven where it was believed to enjoy an eternal existence in a state of glory; it could, however, and did, revisit the body in the tomb, and from certain texts it seems that it could re-animate it and hold converse with it. Like the heart AB it was, in some respects, the seat of life in man. The souls of the blessed dead dwelt in heaven with the gods, and they partook of all the celestial enjoyments for ever.

The spiritual intelligence, or spirit, of a man was called KHU, and it seems to have taken form as a shining, luminous, intangible shape of the body; the KHUs formed a class of celestial beings who lived with the gods, but their functions are not clear. The KHU, like the KA, could be imprisoned in the tomb, and to obviate this catastrophe special formulæ were composed and duly recited. Besides the KHU another very important part of a man's entity went into heaven, namely, his SEKHEM. The word literally means "to have the mastery over something," and, as used in the early texts, that which enables one to have the mastery over something, *i.e.*, "power." The SEKHEM of a man was, apparently, his vital force or strength personified, and the Egyptians believed that it could and did, under certain conditions, follow him that possessed it upon earth into heaven. Another part of a man was the KHAIBIT or "shadow," which is frequently mentioned in connexion with the soul and, in late times, was always thought to be near it. Finally we may mention the REN, or "name" of a man, as one of his most important constituent parts. The Egyptians, in common with all Eastern nations, attached the greatest importance to the preservation of the name, and any person who effected the blotting out of a man's name was thought to have destroyed him also. Like the KA it was a portion of a man's most special identity, and it is easy to see why so much importance grew to be attached to it; a nameless being could not be introduced to the gods, and as no created thing exists without a name the man who had no name was in a worse position before the divine powers than the feeblest inanimate object. To perpetuate the name of a father was a good son's duty, and to keep the tombs of the dead in good repair so that all might read the names of those who were buried in them was a most meritorious act. On the other hand, if the deceased knew the names of divine beings, whether friends or foes, and could pronounce them, he at once obtained power over them, and was able to make them perform his will.

We have seen that the entity of a man consisted of body, double, soul, heart, spiritual intelligence or spirit, power, shadow, and name. These eight parts may be reduced to three by leaving out of consideration the double, heart, power, shadow and name as representing beliefs which were produced by the Egyptian as he was slowly ascending the scale of civilization, and as being the peculiar product of his race; we may then say that a man consisted of body, soul, and spirit. But did all three rise, and live in the world beyond the grave? The Egyptian texts answer this question definitely; the soul and the spirit of the righteous passed from the body and lived with the beatified and the gods in heaven; but the physical body did not rise again, and it was believed never to leave the tomb. There were ignorant people in Egypt who, no doubt, believed in the resurrection of the corruptible body, and who imagined that the new life would be, after all, something very much like a continuation of that which they were living in this world; but the Egyptian who followed the teaching of his sacred writings knew that such beliefs were not consistent with the views of their priests and of educated people in general. Already in the Vth dynasty, about B.C. 3400, it is stated definitely:—

"The soul to heaven, the body to earth;"[1]
and three thousand years later the Egyptian writer declared the same thing, but in different words, when he wrote:—[2]

"Heaven hath thy soul, and earth thy body."

The Egyptian hoped, among other things, that he

[1] *Recueil de Travaux*, tom. iv. p. 71 (1. 582).
[2] Horrack, *Lamentations d'Isis*, Paris, 1866, p. 6.

would sail over the sky in the boat of Rā, but he knew well that he could not do this in his mortal body; he believed firmly that he would live for millions of years, but with the experience of the human race before him he knew that this also was impossible if the body in which he was to live was that in which he had lived upon earth. At first he thought that his physical body might, after the manner of the sun, be "renewed daily," and that his new life would resemble that of that emblem of the Sun-god Rā with which he sought to identify himself. Later, however, his experience taught him that the best mummified body was sometimes destroyed, either by damp, or dry rot, or decay in one form or another, and that mummification alone was not sufficient to ensure resurrection or the attainment of the future life; and, in brief, he discovered that by no human means could that which is corruptible by nature be made to become incorruptible, for the very animals in which the gods themselves were incarnate became sick and died in their appointed season. It is hard to say why the Egyptians continued to mummify the dead since there is good reason for knowing that they did not expect the physical body to rise again. It may be that they thought its preservation necessary for the welfare of the KA, or "double," and for the development of a new body from it; also the continued custom may have been the result of intense conservatism. But whatever the reason, the Egyptian never ceased to take every possible precaution to preserve the dead body intact, and he sought for help in his trouble from another source.

It will be remembered that when Isis found the dead body of her husband Osiris, she at once set to work to protect it. She drove away the foes, and made the ill-luck which had come upon it to be of no effect. In order to bring about this result "she made strong her speech with all the strength of her mouth, she was perfect of tongue, and she halted not in her speech," and she pronounced a series of words or formulæ with which Thoth had provided her; thus she succeeded in "stirring up the inactivity of the Still-heart" and in accomplishing her desire in respect of him. Her cries, prompted by love and grief, would have had no effect on the dead body unless they had been accompanied by the words of Thoth, which she uttered with boldness (*khu*), and understanding (*aqer*), and without fault in pronunciation (*an-uh*). The Egyptian of old kept this fact in his mind, and determined to procure the resurrection of his friends and relatives by the same means as Isis employed, *i.e.*, the formulæ of Thoth; with this object in view each dead person was provided with a series of texts, either written upon his coffin, or upon papyri and amulets, which would have the same effect as the words of Thoth which were spoken by Isis. But the relatives of the deceased had also a duty to perform in this matter, and that was to provide for the recital of certain prayers, and for the performance of a number of symbolical ceremonies over the dead body before it was laid to rest finally in the tomb. A sacrifice had to be offered up, and the deceased and his friends and relatives assisted at it, and each ceremony was accompanied by its proper prayers; when all had been done and said according to the ordinances of the priests, the body was taken to its place in the mummy chamber. But the words of Thoth and the prayers of the priests caused the body to become changed into a "SĀHU," or incorruptible, spiritual body, which passed straightway out of the tomb and made its way to heaven where it dwelt with the gods. When in the Book of the Dead the deceased says, "I exist, I exist; I live, I live; I germinate, I germinate,"[1] and again, "I germinate like the plants,"[2] the deceased does not mean that his physical body is putting forth the beginnings of another body like the old one, but a spiritual body which "hath neither defect nor, like Rā, shall suffer diminution for ever." Into the SĀHU passed the soul which had lived in the body of a man upon earth, and it seems as if the new, incorruptible body formed the dwelling-place of the soul in heaven just as the physical body had been its earthly abode. The reasons why the Egyptians continued to mummify their dead is thus apparent; they did not do so believing that their physical bodies would rise again, but because they wished the spiritual

[1] See Chap. cliv. [2] See Chap. lxxxviii. 3.

body to "sprout" or "germinate" from them, and if possible—at least it seems so—to be in the form of the physical body. In this way did the dead rise according to the Egyptians, and in this body did they come.

From what has been said above, it will be seen that there is no reason for doubting the antiquity of the Egyptian belief in the resurrection of the dead and in immortality, and the general evidence derived both from archaeological and religious considerations supports this view. As old, however, as this belief in general is the specific belief in a spiritual body (SĀH or SĀHU); for we find it in texts of the Vth dynasty incorporated with ideas which belong to the pre-historic Egyptian in his savage or semi-savage state. One remarkable extract will prove this point. In the funeral chapters which are inscribed on the walls of the chambers and passages inside the pyramid of King Unas, who flourished at the end of the Vth dynasty, about B.C. 3300, is a passage in which the deceased king terrifies all the powers of heaven and earth because he "riseth as a soul (BA) in the form of the god who liveth upon his fathers and who maketh food of his mothers. Unas is the lord of wisdom and his mother knoweth not his name. He hath become mighty like unto the god Temu, the father who gave him birth, and after Temu gave him birth he became stronger than his father." The king is likened unto a Bull, and he feedeth upon every god, whatever may be the form in which he appeareth; "he hath weighed words with the god whose name is hidden," and he devoureth men and liveth upon gods. The dead king is then said to set out to hunt the gods in their meadows, and when he has caught them with nooses, he causes them to be slain. They are next cooked in blazing cauldrons, the greatest for his morning meal, the lesser for his evening meal, and the least for his midnight meal; the old gods and goddesses serve as fuel for his cooking pots. In this way, having swallowed the magical powers and spirits of the gods, he becomes the Great Power of Powers among the gods, and the greatest of the gods who appear in visible forms. "Whatever he hath found upon his path he hath consumed, and his strength is greater than that of any spiritual body (SĀHU) in the horizon; he is the firstborn of all the firstborn, and . . . he hath carried off the hearts of the gods. . . . He hath eaten the wisdom of every god, and his period of existence is everlasting, and his life shall be unto all eternity, . . . for the souls and the spirits of the gods are in him."

We have, it is clear, in this passage an allusion to the custom of savages of all nations and periods, of eating portions of the bodies of valiant foes whom they have vanquished in war in order to absorb their virtues and strength; the same habit has also obtained in some places in respect of animals. In the case of the gods

the deceased is made to covet their one peculiar
attribute, that is to say, everlasting life; and when he
has absorbed their souls and spirits he is declared to
have obtained all that makes him superior to every
other spiritual body in strength and in length of life.
The "magical powers" (*heka*), which the king is also
said to have "eaten," are the words and formulæ, the
utterance of which by him, in whatever circumstances he
may be placed, will cause every being, friendly or un-
friendly, to do his will. But apart from any question of
the slaughter of the gods the Egyptians declared of this
same king, "Behold, thou hast not gone as one dead,
but as one living, to sit upon the throne of Osiris;"[1]
and in a papyrus written nearly two thousand years
later the deceased himself says, "My soul is God, my
soul is eternity,"[2] a clear proof that the ideas of the
existence of God and of eternity were identical. Yet
one other example is worth quoting, if only to show the
care that the writers of religious texts took to impress
the immortality of the soul upon their readers. According to Chapter CLXXV. of the Book of the Dead the
deceased finds himself in a place where there is neither
water nor air, and where "it is depth unfathomable, it is
black as the blackest night, and men wander helplessly
therein. In it a man may not live in quietness of
heart, nor may the longings of love be satisfied therein.

[1] *Recueil de Travaux*, tom. v. p. 167 (l. 65).
[2] Papyrus of Ani, Plate 28, l. 15 (Chapter lxxxiv.).

But," says the deceased to the god Thoth, "let the state of the spirits be given unto me instead of water, and air, and the satisfying of the longings of love, and let quietness of heart be given unto me -instead of cakes and ale. The god Temu hath decreed that I shall see thy face, and that I shall not suffer from the things which pained thee; may every god transmit unto thee [O Osiris] his throne for millions of years! Thy throne hath descended unto thy son Horus, and the god Temu hath decreed that his course shall be among the holy princes. Verily he shall rule over thy throne, and he shall be heir of the throne of the Dweller in the Lake of the Two Fires. Verily it hath been decreed that in me he shall see his likeness,[1] and that my face shall look upon the face of the lord Tem." After reciting these words, the deceased asks Thoth, "How long have I to live?" and the god replies, "It is decreed that thou shalt live for millions of millions of years, a life of millions of years." To give emphasis and additional effect to his words the god is made to speak tautologically so that the most unlettered man may not miss their meaning. A little later in the Chapter the deceased says, "O my father Osiris, thou hast done for me that which thy father Rā did for thee. So shall I abide on the earth lastingly, I shall keep possession of my seat; my heir shall be strong; my tomb and my friends who are upon earth shall flourish; my enemies

---

[1] *I.e.*, I shall be like Horus, the son of Osiris.

shall be given over to destruction and to the shackles of the goddess Serq. I am thy son, and Rā is my father; for me likewise thou shalt make life, and strength, and health!" It is interesting to note that the deceased first identifies Osiris with Rā, and then he identifies himself with Osiris; thus he identifies himself with Rā.

With the subjects of resurrection and immortality must be mentioned the frequent references in the religious texts of all periods to the meat and drink on which lived the beings who were believed to exist in the world beyond the grave. In prehistoric days it was natural enough for the dead man's friends to place food in his grave, because they thought that he would require it on his journey to the next world; this custom also presupposed that the deceased would have a body like unto that which he had left behind him in this world, and that it would need food and drink. In the Vth dynasty the Egyptians believed that the blessed dead lived upon celestial food, and that they suffered neither hunger nor thirst; they ate what the gods ate, they drank what they drank, they were what they were, and became in such matters as these the counterparts of the gods. In another passage we read that they are apparelled in white linen, that they wear white sandals, and that they go to the great lake which is in the midst of the Field of Peace whereon the great gods sit, and that the gods give them to eat of the food (*or* tree) of life of which they themselves eat that they also may live. It is certain, however, that other views than these were held concerning the food of the dead, for already in the Vth dynasty the existence of a region called Sekhet-Aaru, or Sekhet-Aanru had been formulated, and to this place the soul, or at least some part, of the pious Egyptian hoped to make its way. Where Sekhet-Aaru was situated we have no means of saying, and the texts afford us no clue as to its whereabouts; some scholars think that it lay away to the east of Egypt, but it is far more likely to represent some district of the Delta either in its northern or north-eastern portion. Fortunately we have a picture of it in the Papyrus of Nebseni,[1] the oldest probably on papyrus, and from this we may see that Sekhet-Aaru, *i e.*, the "Field of Reeds," typified some very fertile region where farming operations could be carried on with ease and success. Canals and watercourses abound, and in one section, we are told, the spirits of the blessed dwelt; the picture probably represents a traditional "Paradise" or "Elysian Fields," and the general characteristics of this happy land are those of a large, well-kept, and well-stocked homestead, situated at no great distance from the Nile or one of its main branches. In the Papyrus of Nebseni the divisions of the Sekhet-Aaru contain the following:—

[1] Brit. Mus., No. 9900; this document belongs to the XVIIIth dynasty.

THE ELYSIAN FIELDS. 179

1. Nebseni, the scribe and artist of the Temple of Ptah, with his arms hanging by his sides, entering the Elysian Fields.

2. Nebseni making an offering of incense to the "great company of the gods."

3. Nebseni seated in a boat paddling; above the boat are three symbols for "city."

4. Nebseni addressing a bearded mummied figure.

5. Three Pools or Lakes called Urti, Hetep, and Qetqet.

6. Nebseni reaping in Sekhet-hetepet.

7. Nebseni grasping the Bennu bird, which is perched upon a stand; in front are three KAU and three KHU.

8. Nebseni seated and smelling a flower; the text reads: "Thousands of all good and pure things to the KA of Nebseni."

9. A table of offerings.

10. Four Pools or Lakes called Nebt-taui, Uakha, Kha (?), and Hetep.

11. Nebseni ploughing with oxen by the side of a stream which is one thousand [measures] in length, and the width of which cannot be said; in it there are neither fish nor worms.

12. Nebseni ploughing with oxen on an island "the length of which is the length of heaven."

13. A division shaped like a bowl, in which is

inscribed: "The birthplace (?) of the god of the city Qenqentet Nebt."

14. An island whereon are four gods and a flight of steps; the legend reads: "The great company of the gods who are in Sekhet-hetep."

15. The boat Tchetetfet, with eight oars, four at the bows, and four at the stern, floating at the end of a canal; in it is a flight of steps. The place where it lies is called the "Domain of Neth."

16. Two Pools, the names of which are illegible.

The scene as given in the Papyrus of Ani[1] gives some interesting variants and may be described thus:—

1. Ani making an offering before a hare-headed god, a snake-headed god, and a bull-headed god; behind him stand his wife Thuthu and Thoth holding his reed and palette. Ani paddling a boat. Ani addressing a hawk, before which are a table of offerings, a statue, three ovals, and the legend, "Being at peace in the Field, and having air for the nostrils."

2. Ani reaping corn, Ani driving the oxen which tread out the corn; Ani addressing (or adoring) a Bennu bird perched on a stand; Ani seated holding the *kherp* sceptre; a heap of red and a heap of white corn; three KAU and three KHU, which are perhaps to be read, "the food of the spirits;" and three Pools.

3. Ani ploughing a field near a stream which contains

[1] Brit. Mus., No. 10,470, Plate 35.

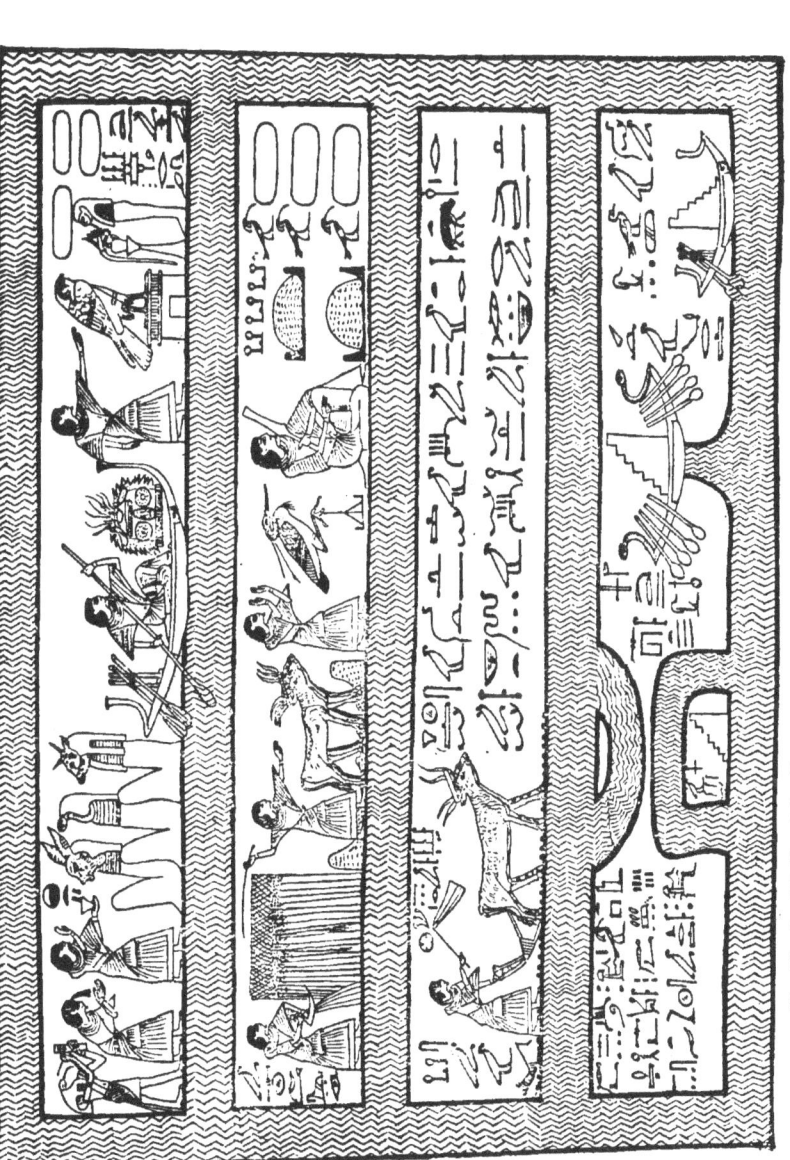

The Elysian Fields of the Egyptians according to the Papyrus of Ani (XVIIth dynasty).

neither fish, nor serpents, nor worms of any kind whatsoever.

4. The birthplace of the "god of the city;" an island on which is a flight of steps; a region called the "place of the spirits" who are seven cubits high, where the wheat is three cubits high, and where the SĀHU, or spiritual bodies, reap it; the region Ashet, the god who dwelleth therein being Un-nefer (*i.e.*, a form of Osiris); a boat with eight oars lying at the end of a canal; and a boat floating on a canal. The name of the first boat is Behutu-tcheser, and that of the second Tchefau.

So far we have seen that in heaven and in the world beyond the grave the deceased has found only divine beings, and the doubles, and the souls, and the spirits, and the spiritual bodies of the blessed; but no reference has been made to the possibility of the dead recognizing each other, or being able to continue the friendships or relationships which they had when upon earth. In the Sekhet-Aaru the case is, however, different, for there we have reason to believe relationships were recognized and rejoiced in. Thus in Chapter LII. of the Book of the Dead, which was composed with the idea of the deceased, from lack of proper food in the underworld, being obliged to eat filth,[1] and with the object of preventing such an awful

---

[1] This idea is a survival of prehistoric times, when it was thought that if the proper sepulchral meals were not deposited at regular

thing, the deceased says: "That which is an abomination unto me, that which is an abomination unto me, let me not eat. That which is an abomination unto me, that which is an abomination unto me, is filth; let me not be obliged to eat thereof in the place of the sepulchral cakes which are offered unto the KAU (*i.e.*, "doubles"). Let it not touch my body, let me not be obliged to hold it in my hands; and let me not be compelled to tread thereon in my sandals."

Some being or beings, probably the gods, then ask him, "What, now, wilt thou live upon in the presence of the gods?" And he replies, "Let food come to me from the place of food, and let me live upon the seven loaves of bread which shall be brought as food before Horus, and upon the bread which is brought before Thoth. And when the gods shall say unto me, 'What manner of food wouldst thou have given unto thee?' I will reply, 'Let me eat my food under the sycamore tree of my lady, the goddess Hathor, and let my times be among the divine beings who have alighted thereon. Let me have the power to order my own fields in Tattu (Busiris), and my own growing crops in Annu. Let me live upon bread made of white grain, and let my beer be made from red grain, and may the persons of my father and mother be

intervals where the KA, or "double," of the deceased could get at them it would be obliged to wander about and pick up whatever it might find to eat upon its road.

given unto me as guardians of my door, and for the ordering of my homestead. Let me be sound and strong, and let me have much room wherein to move, and let me be able to sit wheresoever I please."

This Chapter is most important as showing that the deceased wished to have his homestead and its fields situated in Tattu, that is to say, near the capital of the Busirite or IXth nome of Lower Egypt, a district not far from the city of Semennûd (*i.e.*, Sebennytus) and lying a little to the south of the thirty-first parallel of latitude. It was here that the reconstitution of the dismembered body of Osiris took place, and it was here that the solemn ceremony of setting up the backbone of Osiris was performed each year. The original Sekhet-Aaru was evidently placed here, and we are therefore right in assuming that the fertile fields of this part of the Delta formed the prototype of the Elysian Fields of the Egyptian. At the same time he also wished to reap crops on the fields round about Heliopolis, the seat of the greatest and most ancient shrine of the Sun-god. The white grain of which he would have his bread made is the ordinary *dhura,* and the red grain is the red species of the same plant, which is not so common as the white. As keepers of the door of his estate the deceased asks for the " forms (*or* persons) of his father and his mother,' and thus we see a desire on the part of the Egyptian to continue the family life which he began upon earth ;

it goes almost without saying that he would not ask this thing if he thought there would be no prospect of knowing his parents in the next world. An interesting proof of this is afforded by the picture of the Sekhet-Aaru, or Elysian Fields, which is given in the Papyrus of Anhai,[1] a priestess of Amen who lived probably about B.C. 1000. Here we see the deceased entering into the topmost section of the district and addressing two divine·persons; above one of these are written the words "her mother," followed by the name Neferitu. The form which comes next is probably that of her father, and thus we are sure that the Egyptians believed they would meet their relatives in the next world and know and be known by them.

Accompanying the picture of the Elysian Fields is a long text which forms Chapter CX. of the Book of the Dead. As it supplies a great deal of information concerning the views held in early times about that region, and throws so much light upon the semi-material life which the pious Egyptians, at one period of their history, hoped to lead, a rendering of it is here given. It is entitled, "The Chapters of Sekhet-Hetepet, and the Chapters of Coming Forth by Day; of going into and of coming forth from the underworld; of coming to Sekhet-Aaru; of being in Sekhet-Hetepet, the mighty land, the lady of winds; of having power

---

[1] Brit. Mus., No. 10,472.

Anhai bowing before her father and mother.

The Elysian Fields. From the Papyrus of Anhai (XXIInd dynasty).

there; of becoming a spirit (KHU) there; of reaping there; of eating there; of drinking there; of making love there; and of doing everything even as a man doeth upon the earth." The deceased says:—

"Set hath seized Horus, who looked with the two eyes[1] upon the building (?) round Sekhet-hetep, but I have released Horus [and taken him from] Set, and Set hath opened the path of the two eyes [which are] in heaven. Set hath cast (?) his moisture to the winds upon the soul that hath his day, and that dwelleth in the city of Mert, and he hath delivered the interior of the body of Horus from the gods of Akert.

"Behold me now, for I make this mighty boat to travel over the Lake of Hetep, and I brought it away with might from the palace of Shu; the domain of his stars groweth young and reneweth the strength which it had of old. I have brought the boat into the lakes thereof, so that I may come forth into the cities thereof, and I have sailed into their divine city Hetep. And behold, it is because I, even I, am at peace with his seasons, and with his direction, and with his territory, and with the company of the gods who are his firstborn. He maketh Horus and Set to be at peace with those who watch over the living ones whom he hath created in fair form, and he bringeth peace; he maketh Horus and Set to be at peace with those who watch over them. He cutteth off the hair from Horus and

---

[1] *I.e.*, the Eye of Rā and the Eye of Horus.

Set, he driveth away storm from the helpless, and he keepeth away harm from the spirits (KHU). Let me have dominion within that field, for I know it, and I have sailed among its lakes so that I might come into its cities. My mouth is firm,[1] and I am equipped to resist the spirits (KHU), therefore they shall not have dominion over me. Let me be rewarded with thy fields, O thou god Hetep; but that which is thy wish do, O thou lord of the winds. May I become a spirit therein, may I eat therein, may I drink therein, may I plough therein, may I reap therein, may I fight therein, may I make love therein, may my words be mighty therein; may I never be in a state of servitude therein; but may I be in authority therein. Thou hast made strong the mouth (*or* door) and the throat (?) of Hetep; Qetet-bu is his name. He is stablished upon the pillars[2] of Shu, and is linked unto the pleasant things of Rā. He is the divider of years, he is hidden of mouth, his mouth is silent, that which he uttereth is secret, he fulfilleth eternity and hath possession of everlasting existence as Hetep, the lord Hetep.

"The god Horus maketh himself to be strong like unto the Hawk which is one thousand cubits in length, and two thousand [cubits in width] in life;

---

[1] *I.e.*, I know how to utter the words of power which I possess with vigour.

[2] *I.e.*, the four pillars, one placed at each cardinal point, which support the sky.

he hath equipments with him, and he journeyeth on and cometh where his heart's throne wisheth to be in the Pools [of Hetep] and in the cities thereof. He was begotten in the birth-chamber of the god of the city, offerings of the god of the city are made unto him, he performeth that which it is meet to do therein, and causeth the union thereof, and doeth everything which appertaineth to the birth-chamber of the divine city. When he setteth in life, like crystal, he performeth everything therein, and the things which he doeth are like unto the things which are done in the Lake of Twofold Fire, wherein there is none that rejoiceth, and wherein are all manner of evil things. The god Hetep goeth in, and cometh out, and goeth backwards [in] that Field which gathereth together all manner of things for the birth-chamber of the god of the city. When he setteth in life, like crystal, he performeth all manner of things therein which are like unto the things which are done in the Lake of Twofold Fire, wherein there is none that rejoiceth, and wherein are all manner of evil things.

"Let me live with the god Hetep, clothed and not plundered by the lords of the north, and let the lord of divine things bring food unto me. Let him make me to go forward, and let me come out, and let him bring my power unto me there; let me receive it, and let my equipment be from the god Hetep. Let me gain the mastery over the great and mighty word which is in my body in this place wherein I am, for by means of it I will remember and I will forget. Let me go forward on my way and let me plough. I am at peace with the god of the city, and I know the waters, and the cities, and the nomes, and the lakes which are in Sekhet-Hetep. I exist therein, I am strong therein, I have become a spirit (KHU) therein, I eat therein, I sow seed therein, I reap the harvest therein, I plough therein, I make love therein, and I am at peace with the god Hetep therein. Behold I scatter seed therein, I sail about among its lakes, and I advance to the cities thereof, O divine Hetep. Behold, my mouth is provided with my [teeth which are like] horns; grant me therefore an overflowing supply of the food whereon the 'Doubles' (KAU) and the Spirits (KHU) do live. I have passed the judgment which Shu passeth upon him that knoweth him, therefore let me go forth to the cities of [Hetep], and let me sail about among its lakes, and let me walk about in Sekhet-Hetep. Behold Rā is in heaven, and behold the god Hetep is the twofold offering thereof. I have come forward to the land [of Hetep], I have girded up my loins and come forth so that the gifts which are about to be given unto me may be given, and I am glad, and I have laid hold upon my strength which the god Hetep hath greatly increased for me."

"O Unen-em-hetep,[1] I have entered into thee, and my soul followeth after me, and my divine food is upon my hands. O Lady of the two lands,[2] who stablishest my word whereby I remember and forget, let me live uninjured, and without any injury [being done] unto me. O grant to me, O do thou grant to me, joy of heart; make thou me to be at peace, bind thou up my sinews and muscles, and make me to receive the air."

"O Unen-em-hetep, O Lady of the winds, I have entered into thee, and I have shewn[3] my head [therein]. Rā sleepeth, but I am awake, and there is the goddess Hast at the gate of heaven by night. Obstacles have been set before me, but I have gathered together what Rā hath emitted. I am in my city."

"O Nut-urt,[4] I have entered into thee and I have reckoned up my harvest, and I go forward to Uakh.[5] I am the Bull enveloped in turquoise, the lord of the Field of the Bull, the lord of the divine speech of the goddess Septet (Sothis) at her hours. O Uakh, I have entered into thee, I have eaten my bread, I have gotten the mastery over choice pieces of the flesh of oxen and of feathered fowl, and the birds of Shu have

---

[1] The name of the first large section of Sekhet-Aaru.
[2] A lake in the second section of Sekhet-Aaru.
[3] Literally, "opened."
[4] The name of a lake in the first section of Sekhet-Aaru.
[5] The name of a lake in the second section of Sekhet-Aaru.

been given unto me; I follow after the gods, and the divine 'Doubles' (KAU)."

"O Tchefet,[1] I have entered into thee. I array myself in apparel, and I have guarded myself with the *Sa* garment of Rā; now behold, he is in heaven, and those who dwell therein follow him, and I also follow Rā in heaven. O Unen-em-hetep, lord of the two lands, I have entered into thee, and I have plunged into the lakes of Tchesert; behold me now, for all uncleanness hath departed from me. The Great God groweth therein, and behold, I have found [food therein]; I have snared feathered fowl and I feed upon the finest of them."

"O Qenqentet,[2] I have entered into thee, and I have seen the Osiris [my father], and I have gazed upon my mother, and I have made love. I have captured the worms and serpents [which are there] and have delivered myself. I know the name of the god who is opposite to the goddess Tchesert, who hath straight hair and is provided with horns; he reapeth, but I both plough and reap."

"O Hast,[3] I have entered into thee, and I have driven back those who would come to the turquoise [sky]; and I have followed the winds of the company of the gods. The Great God hath given my head unto me, and he who hath bound on me my

---

[1] The name of a district in the third section of Sekhet-Aaru.
[2] The name of a lake in the first section of Sekhet-Aaru.
[3] The name of a lake in the third section of Sekhet-Aaru.

head is the Mighty One with the eyes of turquoise, that is to say, Ari-en-ab-f (*i.e.*, He who doeth as he pleaseth)."

"O Usert,[1] I have come unto thee at the house where the divine food is brought unto me."

"O Smam,[2] I have come unto thee. My heart watcheth, and I am provided with the white crown. I am led into celestial regions, and I make the things of earth to flourish; and there is joy of heart for the Bull, and for celestial beings, and for the company of the gods. I am the god who is the Bull, the lord of the gods as he goeth forth from the turquoise [sky]."

"O divine nome of wheat and barley, I have come unto thee, I have come forward to thee, and I have taken up that which followeth me, namely, the best of the libations of the company of the gods. I have tied my boat in the celestial lakes, I have lifted up the post at which to anchor, I have recited the prescribed words with my voice, and I have ascribed praises unto the gods who dwell in Sekhet-hetep."

Other joys, however, than those described above, await the man who has passed satisfactorily through the judgment and has made his way into the realm of the gods. For, in answer to a long petition in the Papyrus of Ani, which has been given above (see

---

[1] The name of a lake in the third section of Sekhet-Aaru.
[2] The name of a lake in the third section of Sekhet-Aaru.

p. 33 f.), the god Rā promises to the deceased the following: "Thou shalt come forth into heaven, thou shalt pass over the sky, thou shalt be joined unto the starry deities. Praises shall be offered unto thee in thy boat, thou shalt be hymned in the Ātet boat, thou shalt behold Rā within his shrine, thou shalt set together with his Disk day by day, thou shalt see the ANT [1] fish when it springeth into being in the waters of turquoise, and thou shalt see the ABTU [1] fish in his hour. It shall come to pass that the Evil One shall fall when he layeth a snare to destroy thee, and the joints of his neck and of his back shall be hacked asunder. Rā [saileth] with a fair wind, and the Sektet boat draweth on and cometh into port. The mariners of Rā rejoice, and the heart of Nebt-ānkh (*i.e.*, Isis) is glad, for the enemy of Rā hath fallen to the ground. Thou shalt behold Horus on the standing-place of the pilot of the boat, and Thoth and Maāt shall stand one upon each side of him. All the gods shall rejoice when they behold Rā coming in peace to make the hearts of the shining ones to live, and Osiris Ani, triumphant, the scribe of the divine offspring of the lords of Thebes, shall be along with them."

But, not content with sailing in the boat of Rā daily as one of many beatified beings, the deceased hoped to transform each of his limbs into a god, and when this was effected to become Rā himself. Thus in

[1] The name of a mythological fish which swam at the bow of the boat of Rā.

Chapter XLII. of the Book of the Dead [1] the deceased says—

"My hair is the hair of Nu.
"My face is the face of the Disk.
"My eyes are the eyes of Hathor.
"My ears are the ears of Ap-uat.
"My nose is the nose of Khenti-Khas.
"My lips are the lips of Anpu.
"My teeth are the teeth of Serqet.
"My neck is the neck of the divine goddess Isis.
"My hands are the hands of Ba-neb-Tattu.
"My fore-arms are the fore-arms of Neith, the Lady of Saïs.
"My backbone is the backbone of Suti.
"My phallus is the phallus of Osiris.
"My reins are the reins of the Lords of Kher-āba.
"My chest is the chest of the Mighty one of terror.
"My belly and back are the belly and back of Sekhet.
"My buttocks are the buttocks of the Eye of Horus.
"My hips and legs are the hips and legs of Nut.
"My feet are the feet of Ptah.
"My fingers and my leg-bones are the fingers and leg-bones of the Living Gods." [2]

And immediately after this the deceased says

[1] See *The Chapters of Coming Forth by Day*, p. 93.
[2] The idea of the deification of the human members was current already in the VIth dynasty. See *Recueil de Travaux*, tom. viii. pp. 87, 88.

"There is no member of my body which is not the member of a god. The god Thoth shieldeth my body altogether, and I am Rā day by day."

Thus we see by what means the Egyptians believed that mortal man could be raised from the dead, and attain unto life everlasting. The resurrection was the object with which every prayer was said and every ceremony performed, and every text, and every amulet, and every formula, of each and every period, was intended to enable the mortal to put on immortality and to live eternally in a transformed glorified body. If this fact be borne in mind many apparent difficulties will disappear before the readers in this perusal of Egyptian texts, and the religion of the Egyptians will be seen to possess a consistence of aim and a steadiness of principle which, to some, it at first appears to lack.

THE END.

www.ingramcontent.com/pod-product-compliance
Lightning Source LLC
Chambersburg PA
CBHW041538190426
43193CB00048B/2937